MW00697146

There are three forms of visual art:
Painting is art to look at, sculpture is art
you can walk around, and architecture is
art you can walk through.   --Dan Rice

The Marcellus Williams House (Amelia Island Williams House Bed & Breakfast)

Historic Homes & Buildings of

Amelia Island

Cumberland Island

St. Marys

Fort George Island

Jan H. Johannes

Lexington Ventures, Inc.
Publisher
Fernandina Beach, Florida

Copyright 2002 by Jan H. Johannes. All rights reserved.

No part of this publication may be reproduced or transmitted in any form or by any means
electronic or mechanical, including photocopy, or any information storage and retrieval system
now known to be invented, without permission in writing from the author, except by the reviewer
who wishes to quote brief passages in connection with a review written for inclusion in a
magazine, newspaper, or broadcast.

Library of Congress Control Number 2002094020
Johannes, Jan H., 1940-
Tidewater Amelia : Historic Homes & Buildings / Jan H. Johannes
ISBN 0-9677419-2-0
1. Amelia Island. 2. Cumberland Island. 3. St. Marys, Georgia. 4. Fort George Island.

Published in the United States of America
Lexington Ventures, Inc.
107 Centre Street
Fernandina Beach, Florida 32034

Printed in China through Asia Pacific Offset, Inc.
Offices at
1332 Corcoran Street NW, Suite 6
Washington, D.C., 20009

Photography by Jan H. Johannes

10 9 8 7 6 5 4 3 2 1

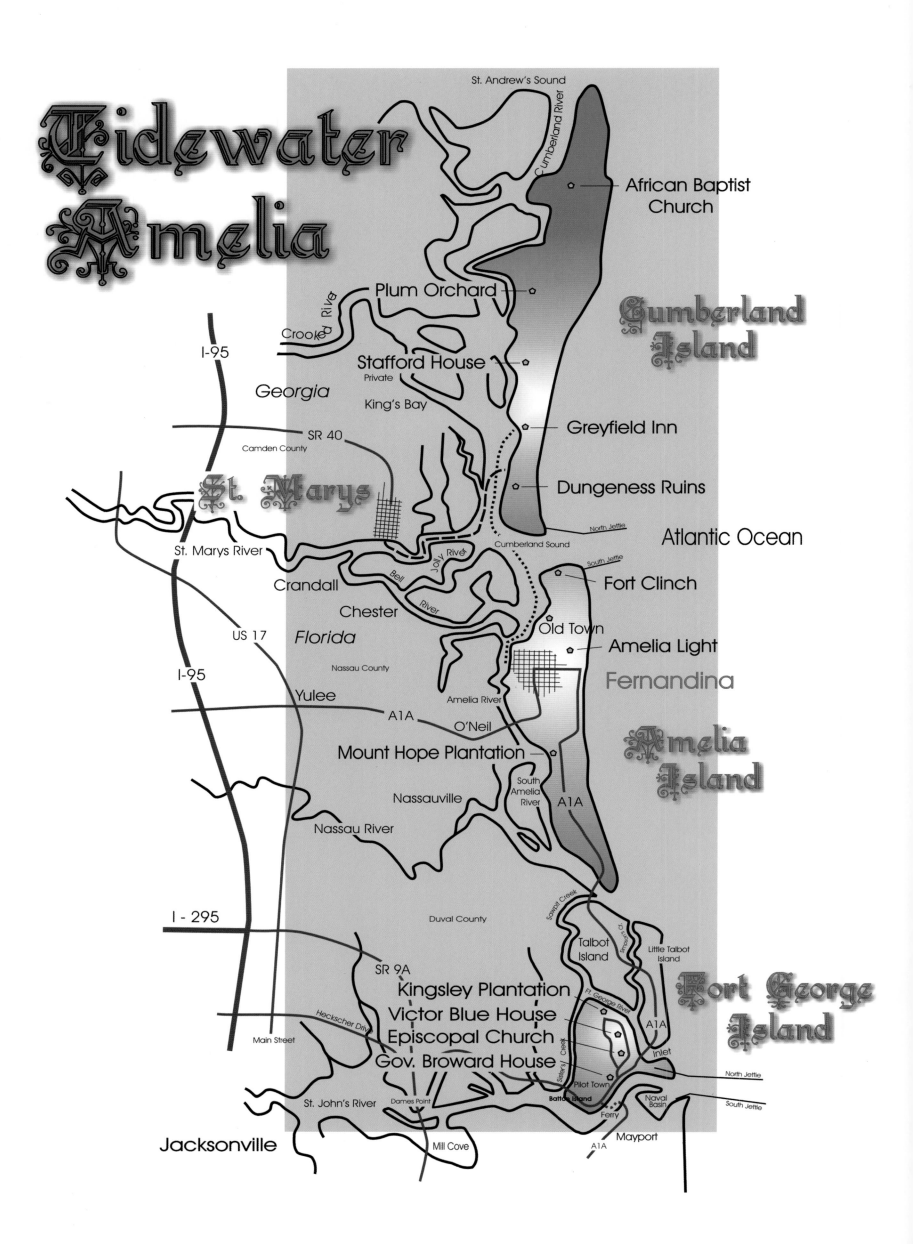

Tidewater Amelia

St. Andrew's Sound

African Baptist Church

Cumberland River

Cumberland Island

Plum Orchard

Crooked River

I-95

Stafford House

Private

Georgia

King's Bay

Greyfield Inn

SR 40

Camden County

St. Marys

Dungeness Ruins

St. Marys River

North Jettie

Atlantic Ocean

Cumberland Sound

South Jettie

Crandall

Bell River

Jolly River

Fort Clinch

Chester

Old Town

US 17

Florida

Amelia Light

I-95

Nassau County

Fernandina

Yulee

A1A

Amelia River

O'Neil

Amelia Island

Mount Hope Plantation

Nassauville

South Amelia River

A1A

Nassau River

I - 295

Duval County

Sawpit Creek

Talbot Island

Little Talbot Island

Fort George Island

SR 9A

Kingsley Plantation

Ft. George River

Victor Blue House

Heckscher Drive

Episcopal Church

A1A

Main Street

Gov. Broward House

Inlet

Sister's Creek

North Jettie

Pilot Town

Naval Basin

Batton Island

South Jettie

St. John's River

Dames Point

Ferry

Mayport

Jacksonville

Mill Cove

A1A

CONTENTS

Dedicated to my wife
Lynne L. Johannes
for her patience and understanding

and to all of you who have
given so much of your lives
to the preservation
and guardianship of
these monuments to the past.

FOREWORD

At the turn into the 20th century, the whispering pines above the islands that stretched along the south-Georgia and north-Florida seaboard sheltered the daily lives and dwellings of the tidewater residents. Within these pages you will view what has come to pass with these wonderfully nostalgic structures that went up a hundred or more years ago on Amelia, Cumberland, and Fort George Islands, and in the 18th century community of St. Marys, Georgia. You will view how dedicated individuals have preserved and adapted the buildings to fit today's life styles.

In a sense, this work is a continuation of my history of Nassau County, *Yesterday's Reflections II,* a photographic history that has enjoyed five printings since its initial release in 1976. There I tell a story in picture and words, of how it all began – what life was like when, what we call history today actually occurred. *Tidewater Amelia* looks at many of those old homes and buildings in the coastal area that have stood the test of time, remaining as monuments to the 18th to early 20th century inhabitants. There are so many homes in St. Marys and on Amelia Island dating from the 19th century that only a select number are featured herein.

Amelia, Cumberland, and Fort George are sister islands of this work due to the unique relationship that has bonded them over the past several hundred years. The catalyst has always been in the commercial and transportation community at Fernandina on Amelia Island, and its central proximity to the neighboring islands. Its early Spanish and British seeds were sewn hundreds of years ago which gave Amelia Island its big-sister status. St. Marys always held a close bond with both Cumberland and Amelia islands.

As with family, the two communities of St. Marys and Fernandina have provided the sister islands with provisions and protection for several hundreds of years. Early forts provided security from unwanted guests, sometimes successfully, occasionally not. Its doctors gave care to those in need, its shipping and industrial interests provided a livelihood, and its stores and warehouses kept supplies in barns and pantries.

St. Marys and Fernandina have been both friend and foe. The two communities are but a few miles across the St. Marys River delta, but two hundred years ago they were many more miles apart when Amelia and, therefore, Fernandina were going through troubled times. Slavery and a Spanish government in Florida kept the two communities at odds until the U.S. Government put both of its feet down on the shenanigans that were taking place in Florida and especially the northeast corner known now as Nassau County.

A natural bond between all of these communities and islands is of course their connection with the sea. Cumberland and Amelia are the two most southerly barrier islands, normally a title associated only with Georgia and the Carolina's. Fort George is a sea island as it is technically a part of the mainland set apart by the inland waterway.

Though Fernandina did not receive its name officially until 1811, the maritime communities of St. Marys and Fernandina have survived since the days of the American Revolution. St. Marys has served Fernandina and up-river St. Marys River communities with ships, crews, and their captains, and her docks have seen many tall-masted ships loaded with timber, ties, resin, and crops shipped to all sections of the world. The St. Marys Railroad connected that community with the major north-south mainline tracks in the interior to keep the community competitive in the commercial world.

Fernandina has profited as a deep-water port since shipping came to the coast more than 200 years ago. The short three miles to the open sea attracted pirates of old, sailing and steam merchant vessels, and today attracts large container ships exporting pulp and paper products around the world.

Cumberland and Fort George Islands appear pristine in a modern world so near, yet so far. Fort George Island, many years ago, saw half of its forests cut and farmed in the antebellum plantation system, but has since returned to lush forest with most of its land overseen by the Florida and National Park Services. Cumberland Island has seen the same evolution of the plantation system but today has returned to the wild. The greatest percentage of its land is today protected under the guardianship of the National Park Service.

In using this publication as a "tour guide," please be respective of the privacy of home owners and the sites under the care of the national and state park services. Leave these precious historic sites as you've found them.

And finally, for the sake of historic clarity, Fernandina Beach is simply referred to as "Fernandina" in most of this publication. The word "Beach" was not added until the 1950's.

Enjoy!

Chimneys Of Amelia
and Cumberland Islands

ACKNOWLEDGMENTS

There are many to thank for their assistance in completing this work. It has been two years in the making in which I have relied heavily on the trust, knowledge, and experience of others.

Donald Shaw, under the name Lexington Ventures, Inc., is the publisher that provided the opportunity and resources that enabled *Tidewater Amelia* to become a reality, and the friendship that saw me through its completion. Jack Heard provided the original concept, inspiration, and endless positive encouragement. The Amelia Island Museum of History once again came through providing me with gracious hospitality and outstanding assistance through the use of their archives. Thanks to David Mallery, Ron Kurtz, Bonnie Sovereign, Marlene Schang, Lori Sage Duerden, Susan Parry, Stacy Osborne, and Carmen Godwin. Thanks also to Harold J. "Hal" Belcher whose brain I picked from time to time on the subject of the Amelia Island lighthouse and other history tidbits.

I would like to give special recognition to my companion, friend, and photographic project assistant who made my daily trips to the tidewater area more fun than work. He reminded me of the things I was about to forget, made suggestions that I hadn't thought of, set up cameras and lights, and was always there when I needed him. This trusted confidant is my grandson, Patrick Ryan McLean.

Many thanks to my wife, Lynne Johannes, who oversaw and edited the text; Kathleen Davis, Cara Curtain, Bob and Agnes White, Suzanne Hardee, Lorraine Petelle, and Jennifer McLean who read and made manuscript recommendations. Thanks to my son, Thomas Johannes, for graphic assistance on the cover. Thanks to Larry Bechan and Deborah Ballou of Fernandina for their technical production assistance, and thanks to James Gleason and Andrew Clarke at Phoenix Offset, printers of *Tidewater Amelia*, for their guidance and coordination efforts.

Thank you George Davis and Leroy McKee for sharing your knowledge of Fernandina and Old Town. Thank you Celeste Kavanaugh who always was there with a smile and a word of encouragement.

Special thanks to Zachary Zoul, Manager of Cumberland Island's Greyfield Inn for all of the amenities afforded me to complete my work on that island; Pamela Sass and Linda F. Howison at the Fernandina Beach Greyfield office; the Carnegie descendents who now are the guardians of Margaret Ricketson and Lucy Ferguson's Greyfield. Many thanks to Greyfield Innkeepers Bruce Beckwith and Brycea Merrill for their gracious hospitality; Greyfield's naturalists Mike Womble and Fred Whitehead for escorting Pat and me to Plum Orchard and the Dungeness ruins. Thanks to a multitude of house staffers that I wish I had the space to list. All of their efforts greatly enhanced the Cumberland Island section of this work.

Thanks to Andy Ferguson, Administrative manager at the National Park Service, St. Marys, for his assistance at Plum Orchard, the Dungeness ruins, and the AME church; to John Mitchell, Museum Curator, National Park Service, St. Marys, for his research assistance; to Bryan Peters, Senior Ranger at the Cumberland Island National Seashore; to National Park Service volunteer Bert Rhyne who escorted me to the tabby house at Dungeness and shared his food and water when I carelessly neglected to take ample supplies on a very hot summer day; and to John Wilder at the Plum Orchard site itself. Thanks to Roger Clarke, National Park Service Senior Park Ranger and his wife, Park Ranger Carol Clarke, for their assistance at the Kingsley Plantation.

Thanks to George Berninger, Florida State Park Ranger at Fort Clinch State Park who must be the premier "interpretive park ranger" in the Florida State Park Service.

Thanks to Debbi Britt for her assistance in coordinating my efforts at St. Marys, to Patsy Scott for reviewing the St. Marys section, and to Mrs. Louise Bailey Thompson for sharing her knowledge and recommendations of sites at St. Marys.

Thanks to Debbie Aaron and Nick Kroker at ZZ Toys for their encouragement and suggestions, and to Willie Mae Ashley for her knowledge and friendship. Special thanks to Nancy and Paul Barnes at the Williams House Inn for providing accomodations for quick turnaround photo shoots, and for their friendship.

This book could never have become a reality without the homeowners, innkeepers, stewards, guardians, proprietors, and building and business owners who opened their doors and allowed me to photograph their historic "museum" adaptations to present-day life. They are the heart of this publication:

Joan Altman at the Captain's house; George L. and Sue Balentine at the Bacon-Burns house; Julie Ballard at Villa Las Palmas; Jeannette Banning at the Rutishauser house; Drew Barrett at the Meddaugh house; Dan and Patti Beard at the Amelia House; Tom and Jenny Bishop at the Bailey house; Gayl Blount at the Hoyt house; Pam Brown at the Phelan-Verot house; Granville "Doc" and Servera Burgess at the Humphreys house; Chris Carter and Dick Flitz, previous owners of the Williams house; Ernest and Marie Chaplin at the Lesesne house; Adeline Davis at the Hirth House; Chris Donnelly, Manager of the Palace Saloon; Juanita Fisher at the Lewis Tabby House; Fernandina Beach Postmaster Jim Foster; Bill and Theresa Hamilton at the Fairbanks House; Nancy and Louis A. "Andy" Frashuer at the Victor Blue house; Richard Germano at the Seydel building; John and Donna Gibson at the Addison house; Jack Heard at the Palmer house; Iris and David Jacobsen at the Vaughn house; Minnie Johnson at the Stotesbury house (The Blue Goose); Celeste Kavanaugh at the Hinton Baker, Jr. house; Clinch Kavanaugh at the Sanborne and Hoyt building; Hardee and Lindy Kavanaugh at the Captain Sharpe house; Lester Kenyon at the McNeil house; John and Julie Kummer at the Chadwick house; Linda Larkin Leonard at the Kydd building; Chris Ludlum and Rob Tate at the Ash Street Inn; Bruce and Pam Magyar at the Ferreira house; Neil and Kathie McGuinness at the Duryee house; Memorial United Methodist Church staff at the Horsey house; Jim Michaels and Scott Palmer at the Prescott house; Mike and Mary Neff at St. Mary's Spencer House; J. M. "Chip" Oxley, Jr., Clerk of Courts at the Nassau County Courthouse; Scott and Rhonda Pursol at the Daniel Kelly house; Greg and Debbi Roland at the Gideon Palmer house; Ron and Casey Sapp at the Richardson-Hardee house; John and Vicki Savino at the Kelly-Swann house; Dr. Robert and Denise Scheffer at the Waas house; Val Schwec at Merrow house (Nassau Terminal); Bob Selton at the Chandlery; Donald Shaw at Fernandina's Schoolhouse Number One; Elizabeth Smiddy at the Bell house (Beech Street Grill); Julie Starr-Sanford at Blue House in Old Town; John and Jan Van Tomme at the Patrick Kelly house; Deborah Watford at Lucy's Cottage; Bob and Karen Warner and Jeanine Rowe at the Florida House; and Carl and Tracy Zillgitt at the Broward house.

Last, but certainly not least, my thanks to all of the clergy and staff of the historic churches for allowing me to photograph their sanctuaries.

ARCHITECTURAL STYLES CONSTRUCTION METHODS & GLOSSARY

Tidewater Amelia is a pictorial overview of historic homes and buildings that have survived into the 21st century. It is not an attempt at scholarly architectural research nor a work of startling discovery. It is a photographic inventory, an account and description of selected structures. Within the following pages is a brief description of architectural styles, notes on those who designed and built them, construction methods and materials used, and a definitive architectural terminology index. With that said, it is hoped that in a small way *Tidewater Amelia* stimulates a greater appreciation of these historic artifacts. It is vital to their preservation that we treasure and respect the architectural gems of our past, for when these are gone, there are no more.

Whether one is involved in restoration, guardianship, or is an observer and admirer of historic architecture, it is hoped that *Tidewater Amelia* will give you a renewed appreciation of the masterpieces that have survived. *Tidewater Amelia's* primary message is to share the interiors of these grand old structures where the Carnegie, Swann, Fairbanks, Kelly, Richardson, Palmer, Borden, Kingsley, and all of the early pioneer families of Amelia's tidewater area lived out their lives.

These were the homes of the elite, community leaders, doctors, railroad workers, merchants, and the common folk. *Tidewater Amelia* will show you the grandeur of Cumberland Island, the simplicity of Fernandina's vernacular, and the embellishment that was the Victorian era. It is the Colonial, antebellum, Victorian-era architecture that *Tidewater Amelia* is all about.

Architectural Styles

The vast majority of historic homes that remain and are photographed in *Tidewater Amelia* were constructed in the late antebellum period (pre-Civil War) down through the early years of the 20th century. This was a time known as the Victorian era that basically encompassed 1850 to 1910. Queen Victoria assumed the crown of England in 1837 and died in 1901, highly influencing various styles of her time, one of them being architecture.

Previous architectural periods partially survived into the Victorian-era which retained some popular trends of roof, window, and fanciful embellishments. Those were the Colonial period from 1670 to 1735, the Georgian period from 1735 to 1790, the Federal period from 1790 to 1820, and the Greek Revival period from 1820 to 1860, overlapping into Victoria's era. St. Marys retains some of the Federal and Greek Revival architecture from the early 1800's, but because of the 1850's relocation of the town of Fernandina a mile to the south, homes and buildings there do not predate 1850. The old original town of Fernandina today has but a few homes remaining from its early 1800 period, most having been destroyed by time, weather, and abandonment.

Within the Victorian era, just to confuse matters, there were a number of architectural fashions that flourished throughout the United States and are evident in many buildings of the Amelia tidewater area. These are the Victorian fashions most noteworthy to this area.

Gothic Revival	Greek Revival	Classical Revival (Georgian)
Italianate	Shingle	Colonial Revival
Second Empire	Folk Victorian	Eastlake
Queen Anne	Stick	

The oldest of Victorian fashion is **Gothic Revival,** appearing from about 1840 to 1880 with characteristics of medieval castles and cathedrals and is found in both ecclesiastical and residential architecture. It is defined by steeply pitched roofs, highly decorated vergeboards along the roof's edge, and tall lancet windows. In churches there are lancet or arch-shaped windows, buttressed walls, and towers, often with castellated parapets. Its growth in popularity came about the same time as the romantic movements in music, plays, and novels of the 19th century. This is the story-book style of Victorian architecture based on English and French precedents from the late 12th to 15th centuries. Though Fernandina has a number of residential buildings with typical features of the Gothic Revival, there are no pure examples remaining. The finest ecclesiastical example in the area is Fernandina's St. Peters Episcopal Church at North 8th Street and Atlantic Avenue. **Carpenter's Gothic** is recognized by its abundance of sawed details. The fact that most of these details were originally designed to be executed in stone did not deter architects and builders from doing them in pine.

The Southern grace of Orange Hall and the First Presbyterian Church of St. Marys, at one time pastored by Horace Pratt, first owner of Orange Hall.

The next fashion was **Italianate,** inspired by large country villas of northern Italy and popular from 1850 to 1890. The style is characterized by a rectangular mass of the body of the house, arranged picturesquely into asymmetric blocks that imitate the sprawling look of centuries-old villas in Italy. Most have been modified and enlarged by many generations. The homes feature low-pitched, often flat roofs, heavy supporting and often elaborately carved brackets under the eaves, and windows with heavy hoods. They most often feature a square tower or cupola, sometimes referred to as "Tuscan." Two examples of Italianate brilliantly stand out on Amelia Island - the Fairbanks house and the Hirth house.

The **Second Empire** style was fashionable about the same time period as Italianate but was somewhat rare in the South. Its most distinguishing characteristic is the mansard roof spotted with dormer windows, as seen on St. Michael's School (formerly St. Joseph's Academy) in Fernandina. Colored tile patterns on the roof and iron crestings were often seen as a part of this style. The American version of the mansard roof comes from the French who created it to circumvent French building codes that prohibited structures above a certain height. The code apparently interpreted the base of the roof as the legal height of the building, allowing owners to mask an additional top floor within the steep roof-like appearance of the mansard design.

The most popular of Victorian architectural style among the middle income and wealthy was **Queen Anne** which dominated residential architecture from 1880 to about 1910. There are various degrees of the style from the modest to the most elaborate which some characterize as a bewildering excess, featuring towers, turrets, porches, balconies, stained glass, roof finials, wall carvings, patterned shingles, elaborate brackets, bannisters and spindles, multiplane roofs, and finely crafted chimneys. Though descended from an English architectural style of the 17th century known as Jacobean, the elaborate versions of the style are more of an American product than its predecessors.

Queen Anne was such a popular style that many older homes were modified to take on its appearance such as Fernandina's Archibald Baker house and the Dr. William. T. Wass house. One of the finest examples of pure Queen Anne is the Bailey House on Fernandina's South 7th Street, built in the early 1890's, and the early 1880's version of Carnegie's Dungeness (now gone but pictured in the Cumberland chapter).

The **Greek Revival** style appeared primarily in residential homes and was an important influence on the architecture of the tidewater area in the decade prior to the Civil War. These homes are rectangular in shape, with low-pitched gabled roofs on the shorter side of the building, the gable usually paralleling the street. There commonly was a full-width porch supported by prominent square or rounded columns. The front door is often surrounded by narrow sidelights and a rectangular transom light. The antebellum Lesesne house at 415 Centre Street and the Florida House on South 3rd Street are good examples.

Variations of Greek Revival were built on narrow street-front lots that extended deep into the center of the block. There the gable faces the street, usually having two stories with full pediments and entrances with sidelights and transoms. Most often seen with offset entrances, others have center entries that emphasize symmetry. Fernandina's First Presbyterian Church is an example.

The **Shingle style** is completely an American innovation that was born out of wealthy Americans desiring rustic rather than formal designs in their vacation cottages. Many examples of the style, popular in the 1880 to 1900 period, were completely covered with shingles, but as the style filtered to the middle class, they resorted to fewer exterior walls covered with the material because of upkeep costs. The style features little to no further external fancy decoration as the shingles are decorative in themselves. The porches are roomy and there usually is a complex roof line and an occasional tower. The Swann Kelly house on Fernandina's South 7th Street is a good example of the style, however, many homes in the tidewater area are decorated with various amounts of shingle.

The most common of Victorian style is **Folk Victorian** as this was the style of the common folk without the luxury of an architect and all of the exotic and fanciful embellishments of the elite. Still many that shared the desire of Victorian design could have their dream homes using local carpenters or their own talents as a means to join the craze. Depending on their experience and creativity, designs were generally less exotic yet still charming. Many of these homes were adorned with flat, jigsaw cut trim in a variety of patterns rather than doweled spindles. They do not have towers, bay windows or elaborate mouldings. It borrows its designs from other Victorian styles in the steep roof of Gothic Revival, or the facade decorations of the Stick style. Today, Folk Victorian is very much symbolic of the mainstream of Victorian architecture with examples numbering in the hundreds throughout the tidewater area.

The **Stick** style is sometimes considered to be only a High Victorian elaboration of Gothic Revival or a transition style between the Gothic Revival and the Queen Anne. It has high pitched and gabled roofs with the gables commonly showing decorative trusses at their peaks. They contained overhanging eaves usually with exposed rafter ends or brackets. They also have wood wall-cladding shingles or boards, interrupted by patterns of horizontal, vertical or diagonal stick work raised from the wall surface for emphasis. This style flourished in house pattern books of the 1860's and 1870's, but carried on til the 1890's.

The **Classical Revival** or **Georgian** style is based on the architecture of ancient Greece and Rome and was one of the most widespread styles in the United States during the late 1800's and early 1900's. Its versatility was adaptable to a wide range of building types and budgets. Plum Orchard on Cumberland Island is a marvelous Classical or Georgian style being restored to its turn-of-the-20th-century elegance.

A revival of interest in the architecture of colonial America occurred between the 1880's and World War II and was appropriately called **Colonial Revival**. The style combines elements of both Federal and Georgian architecture, which were popular styles in America in the 1700's and early 1800's. These buildings were usually formal and symmetrical, some being exact replicas of Federal buildings. The architectural details and massing are distinguished by their large proportions.

The Palladian (three part) window became a standard feature of this new style. Porches with classic columns were used in the finest Colonial Revival buildings, as well as on more modest houses. Elaborately paneled doors topped by fanlights or pediments, and heavy moldings called entablatures ran under the roofs. Windows were the elegant Palladian style, bull's eye (round) windows, or had multiple panes in the top sash and one big pane in the bottom sash. Paint colors returned to the chaste white or light yellows of the Federal era.

The **Eastlake style** refers to both Charles Eastlake, an English architect who advocated the use of wooden decoration, and the use of wooden "stick work" wood construction. Its characteristics are decorative wooden planks (or "stick work") which outline the underlying wood frame structure and intricate wooden details, such as lathe-turned spindles and jigsaw-cut brackets. The finest example of Eastlake is the Bell house at Fernandina's South 8th and Beech Streets.

Architects and Contractors

As the larger organized communities of this coastal area, Fernandina and St. Marys had a number of contractors but few architects to design and construct the homes and commercial districts of their communities. Most buildings did not involve architects but were designed by contractors, carpenters, or in many cases, the owner. These homes or buildings are commonly referred to as vernacular buildings, their designs influenced by local tradition.

The elaborate homes and estates of the affluent were, in many cases, designed by well-known "out of town" architects experienced in upscale design. Skilled and unskilled laborers who built the structures were hired locally and in many cases were employed in maritime related jobs.

Fernandina's architect of distinction in the late 19th century was Robert S. Schuyler, a New York born veteran of the Civil War, who came to Waldo, Florida in 1878 and to Fernandina about 1881. He designed several early Florida churches before coming to Fernandina which still grace the Florida landscape. In Fernandina, Schuyler designed the Fairbanks house, the Lewis (Tabby) house, Public School No.1, St. Peters Episcopal Church, and many others. Characteristic of his unique works were massive and inspiring walls (Tabby house and St. Peters Episcopal), and towering villas (Fairbanks house). Yet he showed an ability to paste intricate gingerbread lace into Carpenter Gothic chapels at Waldo, Fairbanks, and Lake Santa Fe, Florida.

One of Fernandina's most reputable builders was John R. Mann, another veteran of the Civil War, who came to Fernandina in 1881 and built the Humphreys, Hinton Baker, Horsey, and Hoyt houses. He also constructed Villa Las Palmas, the A. S. Allan building, the Methodist Church, and Centre Street's old Keystone Hotel. He assisted on the Nassau County Courthouse, the second Dungeness on Cumberland Island and a number of others. His brother was the primary contractor on the Nassau County Courthouse.

Other builders were Geo. Watts, Frederick W. Plumb, J. B. Van Ness, Wm. Rivers, J. G. Freeman, Geo. Chase and James McGiffin. Van Ness did the Queen Anne Dotterer house on N. 6th Street across from the Presbyterian Church, now gone.

Information on St. Marys contractors is somewhat sketchy, although L. P. Frohock, who lived in St. Marys, was a senior carpenter on Cumberland Island and built a number of homes in St. Marys.

Cumberland Island contractors and architects, such as those commissioned by the Carnegie family, included Andrew Peebles of Pittsburgh, designing their Dungeness with the firm of

McKenzie and Patterson of Boston as the building contractor. The additions to Dungeness in the 1890's were contracted to the architectural firm of Peabody & Stearns of Boston. They, too, designed Plum Orchard in the late 1890's. The architect of Catherine Greene's Dungeness was Phineas Miller, and most likely involved the use of slave labor in its construction.

Construction Materials

Many materials were used in the construction of homes or commercial buildings but here we look at the major structural materials used predominantly in tidewater buildings of historic interest.

Tabby

Though few buildings or livable homes exist today which are constructed of tabby, at one time tabby held a prominent position as a construction material along the southeastern coast. As one of the early materials used by European settlers, tabby was a mixture of oyster shell, lime, and sand, mixed similar to the way we would mix and use concrete today. Coquina is similar in appearance but is a quarried geological form of shell not readily available or used in the Amelia Island tidewater area.

Historically, the use of tabby was limited to a narrow section of the Carolinas, Georgia, north Florida, and south Texas coasts. Examples of the material, most of which dates from the 18th or 19th centuries, have been found on nearly all the sea islands and adjacent mainland areas from Cape Fear, North Carolina, to St. Augustine, Florida, and in the vicinity of Corpus Christi, Texas. The vast majority of tabby structures were located on the southern Atlantic coast, centered at St. Augustine and at Beaufort, South Carolina.

The earliest recorded use of tabby-like materials dates to 1580 at Port Royal Island, South Carolina and at St. Augustine about the same year, where the materials were used to produce roof slabs. By the late 1600's, tabby was used in flooring and walls but it wasn't until the British siege of St. Augustine in 1702 that tabby became a major construction material. Prior to 1702, wood and thatch were generally the materials of choice.

The course tabby from the exterior wall of one of the slave quarters at Kingsley plantation.

At St. Augustine, tabby and coquina had similar developmental histories, with the two materials assuming widespread use from 1702 to 1764. Coquina was more expensive with tabby being the material of choice. The two centers of tabby construction were St. Augustine and north at St. Simons Island where General Oglethorpe built a fort at Frederica, one of the largest assemblages of tabby construction on the coast. By 1742, tabby and its related construction techniques were well established within the British colonies.

With the treaty of Aix-al-Chapelle in 1748, the British abandoned the fort at Frederica and the town there diminished in size. In 1758, fire destroyed most of the buildings leaving the town deserted. With that, the use of tabby in British Georgia subsided.

In 1763, the Spanish returned Florida to the British. In 1783, the British gave Florida back to the Spanish and the flip-flop of power went on. No new homes were built of tabby in St. Augustine from 1784 until 1821 when Spain signed Florida over to the United States. At old Fernandina there is evidence of some use of tabby but it appears that it was primarily used in the foundation piers, drinking wells, and in other minor roles.

There was a revival of the use of tabby in the 19th century. Fort George Island has the immediate area's largest examples of tabby construction in slave quarters of the Kingsley plantation. Kingsley constructed 32 tabby cabins sometime after his arrival in 1814, building in a semicircular arrangement where

Poured tabby of the south wall of the Lewis Tabby house.

slaves lived in family units, each having a fireplace. After the Civil War's collapse of the plantation system, most of the cabins were partially dismantled to use the tabby in the construction of a boathouse. Kingsley's barn was constructed of tabby, partially of tabby brick and partially of poured tabby. On the island's south end is an unfinished tabby home believed to have been constructed for a Munsilna McGundo about 1855. It is believed to have been built by the island's owner at that time, Charles R. Thompson, who died in 1855 with the house not yet completed. It remains incomplete to this day.

In the area of St. Marys is the John Houston McIntosh sugar cane mill built shortly after 1825. This is a two-story structure built of tabby and wood, housing the first cane mill operated by cattle power. By 1842, a number of tabby structures had been built on coastal Georgia plantations and in towns from Darien to St. Marys. Concurrent with tabby's renewed popularity in Georgia was its diffusion along the Florida coasts. The spread of tabby largely coincided with the establishment or expansion of plantations on the islands and adjacent areas of Florida. In view of the sheer number of tabby structures, the years from 1805 to 1842 could be reasonably termed "the plantation era" in the history of tabby construction.

The onset of the Civil War marked the end of the plantation era and of traditional tabby building. There are a few exceptions to this on Amelia Island. St. Peters Episcopal Church was completed in 1884 and the Lewis tabby house was finished in 1885, both designed by architect Robert Schuyler. These tabby buildings differed from previous plantation era tabbies as they were a poured mixture of shell and portland cement. Only about a dozen tabby structures postdate the Civil War. Other than these structures, the use of tabby was relegated to foundations, chimney bases, water wells, and an occasional barn.

The final blow to all tabby building was the development of concrete block and inexpensive commercial cements. The last date for new tabby construction was in the 1920's. The structures are certain reminders that tabby once offered a viable alternative to wood, brick, and stone construction in the coastal sections of the southern United States.

Longleaf Yellow Pine

Southern longleaf yellow pine, pitch pine, or old growth pine are names given the very popular timber used in the construction of tidewater Victorian homes. The history of longleaf yellow pine began in the South where virgin forests covered nearly 70 million acres of the southeastern coastal plain. Many of the trees reached heights of 175 feet taking from 150 to 400 years to mature.

Because of its unique beauty and strength, yellow pine was used extensively in public and commercial buildings and private homes. Most early homes in the South used yellow pine for flooring, furniture and cabinets, and because of its tremendous structural strength, it was used extensively in large building construction.

The center cut of the yellow pine log, referred to as heart pine, was much in demand. With the coming of the Industrial Revolution, by the turn of the 20th century, yellow pine was near extinction. Exacerbating the situation, massive amounts of timber were shipped to Europe due to shortages there. Today, it is estimated that only five percent of the original longleaf yellow pine forests remain.

It is doubtful that there was a home in the tidewater area built prior to 1915 that didn't use heart pine lumber in some portion of its construction. As you page through this publication you will see that almost every home has beautiful heart pine flooring, balusters, and handrails, with many homes having pine ceilings and walls. Unseen are the studs, rafters, and floor joists, all of heart pine.

Most of the inland communities along the rivers and railroads were founded in the harvesting of longleaf yellow pine. For the better part of a century, towns were born and died by its existance and exhaustion.

What is grown and seen in our forests today are loblolly and slash pines, cousins of the longleaf yellow, that are used in the manufacture of a variety of commercial products.

Brick Masonry

Brick masonry construction largely began in the Amelia tidewater area in the years after the American Civil War. The catalyst of the change, as one may guess, was the threat of fire such as the disasterous conflagrations that consumed large sections of Fernandina's business district in both 1876 and 1883.

Fanciful brickwork on the facade of the 5 Star Bar building.

Brick is man's oldest manufactured product. Sun-baked clay bricks were used in the construction of buildings more than 6,000 years ago. In order to prevent distortion and cracking of the clay shapes, chopped straw and grass were added to the clay mixture.

Around 4,000 B.C., the production of brick in uniform shapes began, and sun baking changed to kiln firing to improve the durability of the brick.

The process of lathe and plaster was applied to masonry or studded walls, as today's standard covers walls with sheetrock. The thin wood, or lathe strips, were covered with a mixture of mortar and fiber for strength, dried, then covered with a fine plaster coat.

Locally, after the Civil War, Samuel Swann manufactured clay bricks up-river on the St. Marys at what was appropriately named Brickyard. The Brickyard kilns produced some of the brick used in the construction of Fort Clinch. Other sites at nearby Callahan and Jacksonville manufactured brick for local use as well.

Large amounts of brick were shipped to the port of Fernandina from the Savannah area and northern kilns. The first brick building along Centre Street was the Kydd building at 3rd Street. Built in 1873, it survived at the eastern edge of the great fire of 1876. Following the fire, burned-out sections of Centre Street were reconstructed using the less vulnerable clay brick.

Cast Iron

Cast iron was a mass-produced, American architectural innovation of the 19th century. Used as building facades, cast iron was cheaper than stone or brick and allowed ornate features to be prefabricated from molds in foundries. This represented an inexpensive way to garnish a structure with a face that was ornate, costly looking and stylish. This first represented classically inspired Italian Renaissance, and later, French architectural styles.

In the late 1800's, one could order from a catalog and quickly assemble and bolt a cast-iron facade to a building's frame. It could be painted any color or moved to another building. It could even be melted down and recycled. The new facades permitted designers to build larger windows on all floors, thus bringing natural light to where there was none.

In the 1850's, the readily available architectural cast iron transformed storefront design, as architects and builders experimented using iron columns and lintels at the ground floor level.

Simultaneous advances in the glass industry permitted manufacturing of large panes of glass at a reasonable cost. The combination of these technical achievements led to the storefront as we know it today - large expanses of glass framed by thin structural elements.

Cast iron came to Fernandina in the years following the 1876 fire, at first decorating North 2nd Street commercial buildings and then a number of Centre Street buildings.

The typical 19th century storefront consisted of single or double doors flanked by display windows. The entrance was frequently recessed, not only to protect the customer from inclement weather but to increase the amount of space in which to display merchandise. In some cases, an additional side door and staircase provided access to the upper floors. Thin structural members of cast iron or wood, rather than masonry piers, usually framed the storefront. The windows themselves were raised off the ground by wood, cast iron or pressed metal panels or bulkheads; frequently, a transom or series of transoms (consisting of single or multiple panes of glass) were placed above each window and door. The signboard above the store front (the fascia covering the structural beam) became a prominent part of the building. Canvas awnings, or in some cases tin or wooden canopies, often shaded storefronts of the late 19th century.

Iron fronts were frequently put onto existing buildings as a way of giving them an up-to-date appearance. Except for expanding the display window area to the maximum extent possible and the increasing use of canvas awnings, few major technical innovations in storefront design can be detected from the 1850's through 1900.

Cast-iron pilasters embellish the facade of the old Island City Market.

Stained Glass

The history of the art and general use of stained glass in windows goes back a thousand years and more, to the Mediterranean and the use of alabaster ornamental window openings. The crude glazing of window openings, however, is traced further back to about 300 B.C. or after the advent of Christianity. Stained-glass windows appeared in architecture artistically and technically in the 10th to 11th centuries and in the age of massive Gothic cathedrals.

Those early windows were simply ornamental, transparent mosaics until a colony of Venetian glass workers in 12th century France devised a process which revolutionized the art of stained glass. The new process consisted of painting the glass with metallic pigments which

Stained glass of Fernandina's St. Peters Episcopal Church.

were then fused into the glass itself, providing a color that would last the lifetime of the glass. The process was used, then installed in the windows of the Church of St. Denis in Paris. It was so successful that picture windows became a necessary part of every ecclesiastical edifice.

The use of stained glass expanded into the Renaissance period of the 14th century and the building of grand cathedrals in Europe and England well into the 18th century. The use of stained glass in this period was rarely used outside of the church.

At the beginning of the Victorian era, in both Europe and America, architects and builders began designing stained glass into homes and commercial structures. In the late 1800's, American glass makers devised a new process they called translucent "milky" glass known as opalescent glass. This new process expanded the variety of glass available to artists, dramatically expanding the art of designing with stained glass.

Stained glass did not appear in the Amelia tidewater area to any degree until after the American Civil War when religious sanctuaries and dwellings entered the third decade of the Victorian period. With several exceptions, places of worship initially installed clear glass, later purchasing the expensive stained glass as finances allowed.

Methods of Frame Construction

Wood frame construction has evolved through three basic phases over the years. The earliest Colonial houses are adaptations of English domestic buildings and used what is called **Post and Beam** construction. This system consisted of a timber frame of vertical posts every six feet or more and horizontal beams mortised to the ends to form a rectangular area or room. The frame in the earliest buildings rested on sills on the ground. The roof consisted of beams and mortise where they joined and were often covered with wood shingle. The floors were dirt and later wood.

The 19th century brought **Balloon Frame** construction, made possible by the availability of structural lumber sawed to uniform sizes. The balloon frame system used vertical wall studs the same height as the building. Generally, however, the studs were two-stories high at a maximum. The balloon wall studs extend from the base of the first floor all the way to the top plate or end rafter of the second floor. Both the wall studs and the floor joists rest on a sill anchored to the foundation. The studs and joists typically are toe-nailed to the sill and nailed to each other. A balloon frame, which is held together entirely by nails, could be erected faster than a post-and-beam frame, the end result was stronger and more apt to be square and plumb, and it was cheaper since less-skilled laborers could be used in the construction.

In the latter half of the 19th century, northern suppliers sold prefabricated balloon-frame homes out of a catalog, any style, size, or number, on short notice. Shipped by rail, the building kits contained milled lumber, building plans, roofing shingles, window frames, doors, hardware, and chimneys. The smallest, one-room house measured ten by twelve feet, while the largest home had two stories with eight rooms, pantry, china closet, hall, bathroom, and four closets. Prices ranged from $175 for the one-room house to $3,500 for the eight-room model.

Balloon frames had one serious drawback. Unless fire stops were installed at the level of every floor, the stud spaces formed what were essentially chimneys from the base of the floor to ceiling, greatly accelerating the spread of fire.

The fire problem led to the development of the **Platform** construction system which was purely an American invention.

Technological advancements and the introduction of the steam saw gave free reign to the platform system, which spread rapidly. Building became less time-consuming and appreciably simplified and cheaper.

In platform framing, the first structure built on top of the foundation is the first floor. The builders then use this floor as a platform on which to fabricate the first tier of stud walls. These are then erected and the next floor platform built on top of them, and so on, until finally the roof joists and rafters are put in place atop the final tier of walls.

The platform frame is known to have been in use as long ago as the 1870's. The technique very quickly replaced previous systems. It has now been under development for more than 120 years and, today, is the most commonly used construction system in North American home building.

Architectural Glossary

Arcade: A series of arches supported by columns or piers. An arcade may stand free; if it is attached to a wall it is called a wall arcade or a blind arcade.

Arch: The spanning of a wall opening by means of separate units (such as bricks or stone blocks) assembled into an upward curve that maintains its shape and stability through the mutual pressure of a load and the separate pieces. The weight of the supported load is thus converted into downward and outward lateral pressures called thrusts, which are received by the solid piers (abutments) flanking the opening.

Balloon framing: Balloon framing is a system of wood frame construction, first used in the 19th century, in which the studs are continuous from the foundation sill to the top wall plate.

Baluster: A short post or pillar that supports a rail, thus forming a balustrade. May be curved or straight.

Balustrade: A row of balusters that are capped with a hand railing. Balusrades are typically used on the roofs of 18th- and 19th-century houses commonly used to surround a flattened central area of a low-pitched hipped roof. This formed what is often referred to as a widow's walk from which sea captains' wives could watch for their husbands' ships, or bar pilots could watch for inbound ship traffic.

Battlement: A parapet with alternating openings (embrasures) and raised sections (merlons), such as that at the top of St. Peters Episcopal Church.

Bay window: A window placed in a projection of an exterior wall of a building when the wall projection extends all the way down to a corresponding projection of a foundation. The wall projection may be rectangular, polygonal or curved.

Board and batten: Wall construction using vertical boards with narrower wooden strips used to cover the joints of the larger boards.

Bracket: A horizontally projecting support, typically ornamental and attached to a wall, for an overhanging structure. The brackets most often seen in residential architecture are those beneath the roof overhang of Italianate houses, of which they are a distinguishing feature.

Bungalow: A small house usually having one and a half stories, a widely bracketed gable roof, and a multi-windowed dormer and frequently built of rustic materials.

Buttress: A mass of masonry built against a wall to strengthen it. It is especially necessary when a vault or an arch places a heavy load or thrust on one part of a wall, i.e., St. Peters Episcopal Church. A flying buttress is set away from the wall but curves into and joins it at the top. Both are common to Gothic style architecture.

Capital: The head or crowning feature of a column.

Castellated: Decorated with battlements such as a parapet with alternating indentations and raised portions. Buildings with battlements are usually brick or stone.

Catslide roof: The extended slope of a gable.

Chair rail molding: A wooden molding placed along the lower part of the wall to prevent chairs, when pushed back, from damaging the wall. Also used in decoration.

Chamfer: Cutting away of the corner where two surfaces come together leaving a beveled edge.

Chancel: The space around the altar of a church, usually enclosed, for the clergy and other officials.

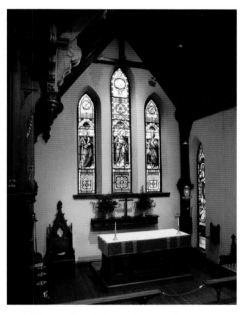

The enclosed chancel area of St. Peters Episcopal Church

Chancel arch: The arch which separates the chancel (sanctuary or choir) from the nave of the church.

Clapboard: Overlapping horizontal boards that cover the timber framed wall of a house.

Column: A pillar, usually round, square or octagonal, used to support the roof of a building, porch, or portico. Parts of a column are the base, shaft, and the capital. Columns are important design elements in Classical Revival and Neoclassical house style. The most traditional columns follow the Greek and Roman orders of Doric, Ionic, Corinthian, Tuscan, etc., and vary primarily in the capital.

Corbel: A stone or timber projection from a wall to support something as seen on the left of the chancel picture above.

Cornice: An ornamental molding, or composition of two or more moldings, located at the exterior wall-roof junction of a building, beneath the eaves, and/or beneath the sloping ends of a gable roof.

Cottage: A small house, usually of only one story.

Cupola: A cupola is a short windowed tower, or dome, typically located in the center of a flat or low-slope roof. Many Italianate houses have cupolas.

Dentils: Toothlike ornaments used in the cornice compositions of main and porch roofs and gables. They occur most frequently on high-style Georgian houses but are also seen on Federal and Classical Revival houses. They can be seen, however, on most styles of architecture in the area.

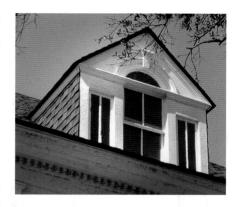

A gabled dormer having sidelights and transom as seen at the Horsey house in Fernandina.

Dormer: A window housed in a gable or similar structure affixed to the sloping part of a roof, providing natural light and ventilation to the rooms beneath the roof. Since such attic or garret rooms have traditionally been used for sleeping, the dormer gets its name from the French verb meaning "to sleep." There are gabled and shed roofed dormers.

Eave: That part of a roof that overhangs the exterior walls.

Eclectic: An architectural design that incorporates several different architectural styles.

Embrasure: Opening in a wall for a cannon such as those seen at Fort Clinch.

Entablature: The horizontal member supported by the columns of a buildings of classic style such as Greek Revival.

Facade: In its most general sense, a facade is an elevation of a building. It is what you see when standing before one side of the building. Under this usage, a house may have two or more facades, a **front facade** facing the street, a **garden facade** facing the back yard, etc. The front facade or principal elevation of a building is sometimes referred to as "the facade."

Fascia: A horizontal piece covering the joint between the top of a wall and the projecting eaves; also called facia board.

Finial: A formal ornament at the top of a canopy, gable or pinnacle, usually in the shape of a fleur-de-lis.

Fluted: Vertical rounded and paralletgrooves usually found on columns or posts.

Frieze: A decorated band along the upper part of an interior wall.

Gable: A triangular wall enclosed by the sloping ends of a ridged roof, or the whole section, including the wall, roof, and space enclosed The majority of tidewater Amelia houses have gable roofs.

Gargoyle: A figurine that projects from a roof or the parapet of a wall or tower and is carved into a grotesque figure, human or animal.

Gazebo: A small lookout tower or open summer house with a view, usually in a garden or park, but sometimes on the porch or roof of a house. Also called a belvedere.

Header: A brick laid in a wall so that only its end appears on the face of the wall. To add a varied appearance to brickwork, headers are alternated with "stretcher," bricks laid full length on their sides.

Hipped roof: A roof in which all four sides are supported by rafters which slope down to the top plates of the walls. Hip roofs are common

A hipped roof can be seen on the left of this Old Town home.

on Georgian and Federal houses, particularly high-style examples.

Hood (window): A decorative projection of masonry or brick protruding out from above a window or door that may be a means of support of the material above the window and, as it implies, shelters the opening below it from the elements.

Joist: Horizontal or near-horizontal structural members of smaller dimensions than beams. Floor joists are the principal underlying element of a wood floor.

Keystone: The central stone which completes the construction of an arch and permits it to carry vertical loads. It is wider at the top than at the bottom and acts like a wedge which used the weight placed on it

The keystone pictured here is part of a window arch covering referred to as a hood.

to force the other block forming the arch together, thus preventing them from falling.

Lancet: A slender, pointed window separated by mullions. Lancets are characteristic of Gothic architecture.

Lintel: A horizontal beam or stone bridging an opening, most often a door.

Mansard roof: This roof is flat on top, sloping steeply down on all four sides, thus appearing to sheath the entire top story of a house or building.

Medallion: A round decorative cover plate at the top of a hanging chandelier or light fixture that covers and protects its connection to the ceiling.

Mortise: A notch, hole, or space cut to join two pieces of wood such as beams or rafters.

Mullion: The vertical element that separates the glass panes of a window.

The mansard roof of St. Joseph's Academy.

Narthex: An enclosed passage between the main entrance and the nave of a church.

Nave: The principal longitudinal area of a church, extending from the main entrance or narthex to the chancel, usually flanked by aisles of less height and breadth, generally used only by the congregation.

Newel Post: A post supporting one end of a handrail at the top or bottom of a flight of stairs.

Niche: A recess in a wall, interior or exterior, often used for a statue. Usually curved at the back.

Nook: A corner of a room or small recess or secluded spot in or from a room. An example is the inglenook pictured at the hearth of Cumberland Island's Plum Orchard estate.

Oriel window: A window placed in a projection of an exterior wall of a building when the wall projection does not ex-

tend all the way to the foundation. In plain view, the wall projection may be rectangular, polygonal or curved.

Palladian window: A window in the form of a round-headed archway with a narrower compartment on either side, the side compartments usually being capped with entablatures on which the arch of the central compartment rests. A typical location for a Palladian window is above the

An oriel window on Fernandina's Centre Street Jeffreys building.

entry door, where it lights an upstairs hallway or stair landing.

Parapet: A low wall placed to protect any spot where there is a sudden drop, such as at the edge of a bridge or housetop.

Pediment: An architectural embellishment used at the top of door- and window-surround compositions. Pediments can take many forms: triangular (peaked like a gable), segmental, or scrolled, etc.

Pergola: An arbor with an open roof of cross rafters or latticework supported on posts or columns.

Piazza: A large covered porch, gallery, or arcade.

Pier: A heavy upright support of floor joists or some segment of a building or bridge. Most homes sat on piers before the introduction of poured concrete slabs.

Pilaster: Pilasters are two-dimensional (flat) ornaments which represent columns. They occur very commonly in 18th- and 19th-century door surrounds. Giant pilasters rising the full height of the facade (usually, but not always, at the corners) are a major feature of many Georgian, Federal and Greek revival houses.

Pinnacle: A pointed termination of a spire, buttress, or other extremity of a building.

Pocket doors: A door, usually one of a pair, that slides into and out of a recess in a doorway wall. Used extensively in the 19th and early 20th century.

Portico: A portico is a roofed area, open to the air on one or more sides, typically supported on one side by the facade of a building and on the remaining sides by columns or arches. Porticos are common on Federal, Early Classical Revival, Greek Revival, and other houses of the 18th and 19th centuries. The English word porch is derived from the word portico.

Post-and-beam framing: A traditional system of wood frame construction in common use into the 19th century in which the skeleton of the house is formed from heavy vertical posts and horizontal beams.

Quoins: The dressed stones at the corner of a building or home, usually laid so their faces are alternately large and small. Usually in contrasting color of brick from the rest of the wall.

Rafter: Structural members that support the roof sheathing to which the outer covering of the roof is attached.

Sacristy: A room in a church, usually adjoining the sanctuary, where the sacred vessels and vestments are kept. Also called a vestry.

Restoration: A representation or reconstruction of the original structure.

Roof: The outside top covering of a structure. There are several basic types of roof designs: gabled, hipped, shed, mansard, and flat.

Rosette: A rose shaped architectural ornament here associated with the box corner of a door or window casing or other framed item.

A rosette corner block at the Fairbanks house.

Rose window: A circular window composed of patterned tracery arranged in petal-like formation usually found in the rear of a church sanctuary, i.e., St. Peters Episcopal Church and Trinity United Methodist Church.

Shotgun house: Originally a simplistically designed house usually one room wide built under a single gable. The entrance is usually on one side of the facade with adjacent windows overlooking the street. This design is of African origin and came to this country in the early 1800's. The reference to shotgun comes from being able to see, or shoot, in through the front door and out the back without hitting anything.

Sidelight: A sidelight is a window found on either side of the main entry door of many Federal, Greek Revival and other late-18th to mid-19th-century houses. ("Light" is a traditional synonym for "window.")

Sill: The lower horizontal part of a window frame. Materials vary widely from wood to marble.

Soffit: The underside of any architectural element as an overhang or staircase.

Studs: In balloon-framing and platform-framing systems of wood construction, studs are the vertical structural members in the walls.

Spindle: A short lathe-turned section of wood such as a baluster. Spindles are found in the ornamentation on hundreds of homes in the tidewater area.

Stucco: Plaster used as a wall covering.

Symmetry: An equal proportion between architectural parts of a building. A balancing of features such as the central location of an entrance on the front of a building. False windows are sometimes built into a wall to give symmetry to the design of that wall.

Tabby: A cement like material made from lime, sand and oyster shells. Its origin is uncertain although early documents record Indian burial vaults with walls made of oyster shells and lime. Early documents suggest that it is likely the 16th-century Spanish explorers first brought tabby to the southeast coast.

Terra-Cotta: A hard, brown-red usually unglazed piece of building material, usually brick size or larger, often cast in in-tricate shapes. The fireplaces of Fernandina's Waas house are a beautiful example.

Tower: A square or octagonal projection from the base of a house or building that rises above the level of the top floor.

Transept: A rectangular area which cuts across the main axis of a basilica-type church and projects out beyond the main structure of the church building. When viewing from

Tower of the Captain's House, Old Town Fernandina.

above, it gives the building the appearance of a cross.

Transom: A small, usually rectangular or fanlight window over the door. Some open to cross-ventilate a home while others are only decoration.

Truss: A number of wood planks framed together to bridge a space.

Turret: A small tower projecting from a building, usually at a corner and often merely ornamental.

Tuscan Order: The simplest of classic orders of architecture, i.e., unfluted columns, simple bases and capitals, and unadorned entablatures.

Vault: An arched roof or ceiling labeled as barrel, tunnel, fan and groin such as those seen at Fort Clinch.

Veranda: a large, open porch, usually roofed and partly enclosed, as by a railing, often extending across the front and sides of a house. Also called a gallery or a piazza.

Vergeboard: A board, often carved, hanging from the projecting or gabled end of a sloping roof. Also called bargeboard.

Vernacular: This term describes an architectural style or design of house derived primarily from popular taste. Vernacular styles usually stem from some more formal or academic style, with simplifications and adaptations, but their origins are still recognizable. Vernacular styles can be found throughout the Amelia Island tidewater area.

Voussoir: Any of the wedge-shaped stones of which an arch or vault is built.

Wainscot: Decorative paneling covering the lower three to four feet of an interior wall. Can be found in many homes no matter the age or style.

Widow's walk: A small, railed observation platform at the top a house. Once used to scout for seaman, such walks are usually square and usually conform to the architecture of the house below.

Amelia Island has been inhabited for thousands of years as have many of the sea islands along the southeast coast of North America. On the northwest end of the island, facing the inland waterway, is a high bluff that offered good visibility for defense of the inhabitants, abundant food supplies, an excellent harbor, and short distance to the open sea. At this bluff, now called Old Town, archeologists and researchers have concluded that humans have inhabited the island for nearly 4,000 years.

The native American tribe of northeast Florida and southeast Georgia was the Timucuan Indian. The Timucuans made their dwellings of round walls and conical roofs, covered thinly with palm leaves and bark. Their storehouses were built of stone and earth with roofs of thickly laid palms and soil.

Then came the French in 1562. The Spanish followed a few years later, and began their occupation of Florida which lasted until 1821. The Spanish established the mission of Santa Maria de Sena on Santa Maria, now Amelia Island, and brought with them dwelling designs of European influence. The attempts toward establishment of an organized community at the bluff on the north end of the island floundered many times through the years.

The English built a fort on the bluff in the 1730's and took possession of Florida from Spain, in 1763, for 20 years. The island was in the midst of unstable times between the English to the north and the Spanish to the south, and would not have been the wisest of choices for peace-loving settlers. The British platted a town west on the St. Marys River, calling it New Bermuda, but sickness and a hard journey from island of Bermuda thwarted that endeavor. New Bermuda was where the settlement of Crandall is today.

During English occupation, 10,000 acres on Amelia were granted to the Earl of Egmont, including the bluff, where he built and operated a plantation. A Spanish map of 1778 depicts a new village on the bluff but its seems more probable that these were simply buildings in support of Egmont's plantation.

The Spanish returned in 1783 and relaxed land ownership laws in the 1790's. This promoted emigration and settlement by both British settlers forced south by the American Revolution and American patriots seeking new holdings, creating a renewed settlement at the bluff on Amelia Island. This immediately increased use of its Amelia River harbor.

Domingo Fernandez received a Spanish land grant on Amelia in 1790 and assumed a harbor pilot position which signaled an increased use of the harbor and a settlement on the rise.

It was during this second Spanish occupation period that the settlement became a town and was eventually organized and platted by the Spanish in 1811. It was named Fernandina to honor the current monarch of Spain, Ferdinand VII.

Buccaneers came ashore, seeking to take control. Slave trading and smuggling intensified then gradually decreased due to pressure from the United States just to the north. In 1821, the United States took possession of Florida from the Spanish and by 1824 Nassua County was formed with its county seat at Fernandina - up on the bluff.

While the town of St. Marys flourished across the river, Fernandina fell into neglect and abandonment. Few homes were built or new businesses started - most closing and going elsewhere. By 1838, the county seat was moved to the mainland where it stayed until the close of the War Between the States. Its life blood would begin pumping again in the 1850's when Fernandina was named the eastern terminus of the new Florida Railroad, the first Atlantic Ocean to Gulf of Mexico rail that terminated to the west at Cedar Key. However, the railroad could not be built across the swamp just to the south of the bluff. It was constructed from what is today the west foot of Centre Street, and the heart of Fernandina followed that shift to its present location.

The little community on the bluff continued to be occupied by harbor pilots and seaman but the new center of Fernandina, at the newly platted site, expanded up Centre Street to the east.

Secession of the southern states occurred in South Carolina in 1861, and by 1862, the Union Navy arrived and occupied the island for the duration of the war. Fort Clinch survived, as well as many homes and a few businesses built prior to the war. It was after the war, however, that most of the surviving architecture today had its beginnings. The Victorian era went into full swing as did the prosperity of one of the finest ports in the Southeast. Amelia's modest, yet very Victorian construction reached its peak toward the end of the 19th century, dwindling until about 1910 when the era became history.

And now a view of Amelia Island's treasures.

The Gothic Revival architecture of St. Peters Episcopal Church, Fernandina Beach.

Reverend Archibald Baker House

Hinton Baker, Jr. House

HINTON BAKER HOUSE

There are two Baker houses adjacent to one another on North 6th Street. The Reverend Archibald Baker home was built in 1859 at 112 North 6th Street. Archibald was the founding pastor of the First Presbyterian Church. It received major architectural changes in the early 1900's such as a veranda and tower which changed its appearance to the popular Queen Anne style.

Next door is the Judge Hinton J. Baker, Jr. house at 102 North 6th Street built circa 1905 by the grandson of Archibald Baker. Hinton J. Baker, Jr. was a prominent attorney in Jacksonville and Fernandina, having served as city attorney and judge,

prosecuting attorney, county attorney, attorney for the school board, and many other institutions of the area.

Architecturally, the Hinton Baker house is a two-story frame vernacular structure eclectic in bits of Queen Anne, Colonial Revival, and Stick styles. Its architectural signatures include brackets under the eaves, shingle ornamentation, irregular wall surfaces, and two prominent horseshoe arches on the facades of the main house and the carriage house. The builder of the Hinton J. Baker, Jr., house was John R. Mann, a well known local contractor.

The Red Room.

The Hinton Baker house has been restored to its original beauty by descendents of the original owner. Oriental chandeliers and numerous other oriental items in the Red and Blue Rooms were gifts to the Hinton Bakers from Chung Li Sing, South 3rd Street gift shop and laundry owner. Heart pine floors, moulding, and other light fixtures are as the Bakers placed them nearly 100 years ago.

Hinton James Baker Jr.
Attorney and Nassau County Judge

The Green Room.

Celeste Kavanaugh
Collection

CHADWICK HOUSE

At 121 North 6th Street is the two-story Queen Anne residence originally belonging to Captain Stephen Chadwick, livery operator and owner of a fleet of tugboats. Architectural features of note are its gable-on-hip roof, its gingerbread, bay windows, and large veranda.

Brass was the Victorian era metal of choice for knobs, hinges, locks, and light fixtures.

The entrance hall is highlighted with the original stained-glass doors, staircase, and flooring, all crafted of virgin yellow pine.

Standing majestically alongside her sister homes in the 100 block of North 6th Street is the Stephen Chadwick House, constructed in 1883 by Captain Stephen Chadwick and his wife Georgia Virginia King Chadwick. Its Queen Anne era architecture was stylish for the period and masterfully constructed of Nassau County virgin heart of yellow pine.

Stephen, and later his descendents have continually occupied the home since the day of its completion.

Stephen Chadwick's ancestors came to America in the 17th century, to Falmouth, Massachusetts, and for many generations sailed as whalers along the New England seacoast. In the early 1700's, three Chadwicks moved south to the area of Cape Lookout near Beaufort, Carteret County, South Carolina. They and their descendents continued as mariners in various capacities such as ship's masters or whaling hands, spending much of their lives on the high seas.

Following the Civil War, Stephen Chadwick, Jr., his brother James, and their older sister Mary came south to the area of the St. Marys River. It isn't known exactly where the Chadwicks first lived but they had strong ties with Kings Ferry, St. Marys, and Fernandina.

The brothers captained tugs operating out of Fernandina with Captain Stephen Chadwick eventually owning and operating three tugs, co-owning the steamer Hildegarde, and having large land holdings that included the 3,500 acre White Oak Tract on the St. Marys River. Stephen's son, Louis Stephen Chadwick, Sr., followed a Chadwick tradition of wise spending and investments, becoming a leading citizen and entrepreneur on Amelia Island and out in the county. He constructed his home at 131 North 6th Street, next door to his parents house at 121 North 6th Street. Many years after his death, that Chadwick home was ordered dismantled by Louis's widow and today remains simply a memory of the past.

Large living and sitting rooms, broad pocket doorway passages and large windows allowed even the lightest breeze to relieve summer heat. The house throughout was trimmed of yellow pine. Richly decorated hearths were the only source of heat for many years, the Chadwicks having two on the first floor and two in the sleeping quarters on the second floor.

The dining room was on the north side of the house where the Captain and his wife could see beyond the carriage house to their son's home on the corner.

The Chadwick porch on the southeast corner of the house gives one a view of North 6th Street and its memory-lane ambience. Many years ago, just outside of the now screened in enclosure, utility workers uncovered the remains of a Confederate soldier.

RICHARDSON - HARDEE HOUSE

First residential record of this property is about 1882 when Samuel Swann purchased lots 14 and 15 from the estate of an A. H. Cole. The next recorded transfer was to Sarah Frisbee, who passed it on in her estate to James F. Johnson.

In 1900, Dr. Percy N. Richardson bought lot 14 and a year later purchased lot 15. The 1903 tax records indicate a $1000 improvement made to the property - an exceptional bargain even at earliest 20th-century prices.

This corner home was built circa 1902 by Dr. Richardson, who was a well-respected African American physician and druggist, prospering in the midst of a turn-of-the-century, predominately white, commercial and residential community. His business was at 18 N. 4th Street.

The Richardson home was sold several times, and by 1905, came into the hands of Everett and Annie E. Johns. Though the Johns family owned and lived in the house but for a short time, it is significant in that their son, Charles E. Johns, became Governor of Florida from 1953 to 1955.

By 1910, the house was purchased by Noble Anthony Hardee who had become partners, in 1900, with brothers Ira and John in the hardware and grocery business operating as N. A. Hardee & Brothers. In 1918, the brothers split the business and founded the Standard Hardware Company which has evolved into Standard Marine Supply on North 2nd Street. Ira ventured into the commercial shrimping industry and real estate, always maintaining his relationship with Standard Hardware.

The home is maintained today as a private residence.

The Richardson/Hardee House is of Queen Anne influence, noteworthy for its ornamental shingles, two-story hexagonal bays, hip roof, ornamented veranda, and a gabled sunburst pediment over the corner of the veranda. Note the false window frame inserted to maintain the symmetry or balance of the overall design.

The sitting room hearth.

Stained glass at the second-floor landing.

The Richardson - Hardee House is a residential vernacular design having heart pine flooring with painted banister and ornate newel post.

DURYEE HOUSE

The carriage stepping stone.

The home of Major William B. C. Duryee is most notable as it was the first house built in new Fernandina following the War Between the States.

Duryee's home previously had been New York City. Prior to settling in Fernandina, he had served in the war as an officer of the Army of the Potomac. He saw carnage on many battlefields of the war, was severely wounded, and subsequently decorated and breveted to Major for his heroism at Antietam.

At war's end, he came south to Fernandina where he took the position of Special Deputy Collector of Customs. At the end of his term of office, he established himself in the lumber business and the retail grain and feed business. He was elected to the city commission, was the acting British Vice-Council, and was a vestryman at St. Peters Episcopal Church.

After reaching some measure of financial success, about 1885, Duryee built a much larger home on the southwest corner of Centre and 8th Streets that has since been razed.

The interior of the Duryee home is both warm and stately. Ceiling heights in the entrance hall and front room are a towering 13 feet. This had been the common height throughout the first floor at one time, but the remainder of the first-floor ceilings were lowered at some point, many years ago.

The dining room bay window is where Mrs. Duryee's ghostly image has reportedly been seen sitting in a rocking chair.

One of Major Duryee's business buildings is at the foot of Centre Street, for many years now the Marina Restaurant.

Major Duryee died in 1913. Mrs. Duryee stayed on in the house until the 1920's before selling and moving north to live with her daughter.

Stories persist, even into modern times, of a ghostly image of an elderly lady, perhaps the major's wife, sitting in a rocking chair at the dining room window causing some to believe that upon her death she returned to the place where she and the Major had lived most of their lives.

Under the ownership of the Stiles family, the dining room was made into a bedroom for an invalid child. That child had a small black dog named "Inkie" who would growl at the sight of the chair rocking with no one in it. Perhaps he sensed Mrs. Duryee's presence.

A showpiece staircase.

JOHN FERREIRA COTTAGE

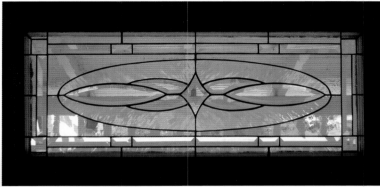

The transom window.

The multi-galleried porch surrounds what otherwise could be considered a Florida plantation house, a simple four room structure with fireplaces at the gabled end of the house. Additions to the rear brought the kitchen into the house. Springtime azaleas light up the landscape framing a postcard cottage.

The Ferreira family were pioneer residents of St. Augustine, coming to Fernandina when young John A. Ferreira was about age ten, just before the Civil War. John began a long career with the Florida Railroad and its successor lines in 1867, as an apprentice in the railroad's Fernandina machine shops. He later was elevated to engineer, regularly making the run from Fernandina to Cedar Key. Ferreira and his engine were assigned to make that same run in 1878 when General Ulysses S. Grant was making his victory tour. Uncle Johnny, as he was referred to, retired in 1918 with 51 years of railroad service.

John and his wife Clementine built and lived in this one-and-a-half-story frame vernacular cottage about the year 1873. Its most noteworthy architectural features are the broad 10-bay veranda with scrolled and bracketed gingerbread decors, a unique baluster design, and its gabled roof.

The cottage's antiquity shows in its box lock, pine floors, and oak mantle.

HORSEY HOUSE
ALSO KNOWN AS
THE DICKENS HOUSE

This was the home of Dr. John Louis and Francis Chairs Johnston Horsey and their children. This two-and-a-half story Queen Anne edifice was constructed in 1902 by contractor John R. Mann using balloon frame construction.

Dr. Horsey was a general practitioner, a druggist and chemist, owning the firm of Horsey & Co., initially with his brother, Dr. Charles W. Horsey, who died a young man. The widow of Charles assumed her husband's half of the partnership with John. This firm began on Centre Street in the two-story building formally owned by Huot & Co., later moving around the corner to 2nd Street. Dr. John Horsey was also the physician in charge of the Marine Hospital once located at 1st and Calhoun Streets.

With the death of John and Francis, the house was acquired by their daughter, Anita, who lived there with her husband, Earl Huntly, for many years. The Huntly children, who grew up in the house, were Earl, Jr., Jane, and Pat.

In later years the house was owned by Dr. Bailey Dickens, a general practitioner, whose name was attached to the house for a number of years.

The Horsey house is architecturally significant for its octagonal turret, its veranda which originally extended around the east side of the house, its hipped roof, and gabled dormers. During the 1950's cold war period, the owner had a bomb shelter built within the house.

Constructed in the late Victorian period, the Horsey house is essentially Queen Anne with its turret, fishscale shingles, and veranda with simple columns and Doric capitals.

The entrance hall leads to the front parlor and dining room and the heart pine staircase to the leeping rooms above. Beyond can be seen the oval stained glass that faces Centre Street.

J. L. Horsey & Co. medicine bottle.

The dining room hearth.

Glass of the tower window.

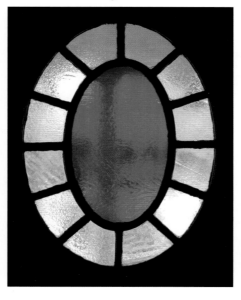

The east-side gabled dormer, unique with double sidelights and transom.

Standing at the corner of North 6th and Alachua Streets is the Louis Hirth house. This lovely house could be called the gateway to Fernandina's golden era of residential extravagance.

HIRTH HOUSE

Original dining area fixtures include the brass chandelier and a stained-glass window in the bay on the south side of the house.

The Hirth House, located at 103 North 6th Street, is in what is referred to as Fernandina's "silk stocking district," meaning that in its heyday, if you could afford the luxury of silk stockings, you could afford to live on North 6th Street.

Designed in the Italianate villa style by Robert S. Schuyler, the house was constructed in 1886 for Thomas Moore, editor of a local newspaper, and his wife Annie.

With the editor's transfer to another city in 1896, the home was sold to Louis G. and Emma Amelia Hirth for $1,800.

German born Louis Hirth had come to America in 1866 and to Fernandina in the 1890's, entering into the liquid refreshment business as a bartender. Before long, he opened his own pub, the Trilby, at 7 North 3rd Street in 1898. In 1903, Hirth helped to write history when he turned a shoe store and haberdashery into his now famous Palace Saloon at the corner of North 2nd and Centre Streets.

Shortly after the turn of the century, Hirth had his home's small original porch removed replacing it with one of colonial revival style. The new porch, or veranda, was similar in design to those at the Humphreys and Baker houses in the same block. Louis and Emma Hirth, raised four children in this home, three girls and a boy.

Hirth's granddaughter, Adeline Davis, and her husband, George, acquired the home in 1972. There followed several years, hundreds of hours of labor, and many thousands of dollars dedicated to the restoration of the structure. With the hurricane of 1898, all of the homes were slightly tilted to the northeast, and remained that way for many years. In the restoration effort, the house was leveled after 70 years of an ever-so-slight tilt. A new roof was installed, layers of paint stripped from the trim, yellow pine floors were refinished, plastered walls were covered with sheet rock and all surfaces were repainted, stained, or buffed. All of the woodwork is yellow pine with the exception of the cherry wood staircase, still adorned with the original newel post "Vaseline glass" fixture.

The front parlor has been meticulously restored, paint stripped from much of the trim revealing the exceptional beauty of the yellow pine. Window trappings exhibit the air of the late Victorian era. The windows are at the base of the two-story bay so well defined on the homes exterior. The parlor measures 18 by 15 feet. A brightly-colored glass chandelier that once hung from the ceiling, now adorns the large kitchen area at the rear of the house.

The setting of the oak mantle of the front sitting parlor retains the two turn-of-the-century imported Italian bird vases ordered by Louis Hirth as original trappings of his Palace Saloon. Emma Hirth saved them from what she called the doom of rowdiness at her husband's saloon, bringing them home for safe keeping where they continue to be watched over by his descendents. The mantles were installed by Hirth in 1905.

The cherry wood staircase and its newel post are adorned with a Vaseline glass fixture. Pine flooring here and throughout the house is covered with a modern material to protect the original yellow pine.

The Vaseline globe softly illuminates the room with the late afternoon light that makes its way through the entry-way glass. The original door glass was replaced in the 1970's with this gift of period art to Hirth's granddaughter.

The original architectural plans called for an eventual addition, which would double the size of the house. Those plans, however, were never implemented, eventually causing Hirth's Italianate castle to be affectionately dubbed "half a house." The entrance hall is now on the north side of the house but, had the addition been completed, would have been through the center of a rather large dwelling.

In the entrance hallway just to the right of the doorway can be seen the business ledger of Hirth's first pub, The Trilby, located on North 3rd Street.

Mixing and matching architectural styles was not uncommon at whatever the price of the home. The Queen Ann style is associated with all that is here, except for the porch. It is Colonial Revival.

HUMPHREYS HOUSE

Another of the North 6th Street gems is the Humphreys house, a two-story Queen Anne style, private residence, designed and built by John R. Mann for Dr. D. G. Humphrey, a prominent local physician with offices at Centre and 3rd Streets. The house is noteworthy for its octagonal tower, hipped roof, and the broad wrap around veranda. It is said that the Humphreys house had the first veranda on the block, and its popularity convinced others in the neighborhood to add their own.

Some of the outstanding features of the interior are its intricate gingerbread work, pocket doors, and three original stained-glass windows strategically placed to catch the rising, noon, and setting sun.

The property was the original location of the R. S. Lukenbill home, another fashionable manor of Fernandina that burned near the turn of the century. The only signs today of that residence are its sidewalks.

The Humphrey House has been restored and preserved by descendents and includes furnishings from the bridal suite of the 19th-century Egmont Hotel.

Gingerbread spandrels help to separate the tower window area from the entry hall, typical of Victorian era design. Yellow pine flooring, trim, and stairways have been masterfully restored and maintained.

A view from the turret through the entrance hall to the front sitting and dining rooms. The staircase, with deeply stained handrails, balusters, and newel posts, reflects the afternoon sunlight that passes through the landing stained-glass window to the grandfather clock below. The staircase adds a great deal of Victorian charm to the entry hall and to the superb restoration that graces the Humphrey House.

The sitting-room oak hearth surrounds the ceramic-tiled firebox as flames warm the air into the dining room. One of three stained-glass windows can be seen in the service nook, just behind the vase of flowers. Fine carpets protect the original pine floors and add warmth to the living area.

The library connects the front entry hall with the rear kitchen and a large living room addition to the original house.

PATRICK KELLY HOUSE

In 1999, a returning Patrick Kelly grandchild recalled her childhood at this house and of learning so much about life sitting at the feet of the family's older generations on pleasant evenings relaxing on the front porch.

The Patrick C. Kelly House was constructed in 1899 and 1900 for Patrick and Angie Kelly. It is a frame vernacular private residence with design noteworthy for its stick-style porch, square bay windows, and unique single-sidelight entrance with a colorful glass transom.

Patrick C. Kelly was the son of Patrick Kelly who had immigrated to America from Ireland and whose legacy centered around his seat in the Florida Senate. The elder Kelly assumed the guardianship of orphaned Angelica Acosta who, in time, married the son, Patrick C. Kelly. Patrick and Angelica built their home across the street from Fernandina's Convent of the Sisters of St. Joseph for the meager sum of $2000. They added an addition several years later that too came at a cost of $2000.

The Kellys raised their children Maurice, Helen, Marcel, Theodosia and Patrick C. Kelly, Jr. here on North 4th Street, along with Angie's old sister May who lived with them her entire life.

There were beautiful flowers throughout the yard, even in the area of the chicken house where the little feathery creatures roamed their own yard. Angie was the gardener in the Kelly family, a love that has passed on to the current guardians of the home in 2002.

Patrick Kelly was the mayor of Fernandina for many years and, with his brother Dan, operated a grocery and marine supply store on Centre Street across from the Palace Saloon. The brothers were instrumental in laying the first roadbed, beyond that of the original old trail, from the mainland onto the island. The Kellys were very successful and active in the social and cultural events of the community.

With the growth of south Florida, the decline of railroad activity on the island, and the devastating economic effects of the late 1920's, the Kelly fortune eventually collapsed along with many other businesses of the time. At the death of Patrick and Angie the house was left to their children. Marcel "Buck" Kelly and his wife Julia occupied the house for many years keeping the house in the family, though the other Kelly children found employment and lived their lives in other parts of the country. The last family occupants, Helen Griffin and her daughter, Helen Elizabeth, remained there until the 1960's when they sold and moved on.

The elegantly polished floors, window and door trimmings are of native heart yellow pine. The entrance hall and parlor reach to ten-a-half-foot ceilings with the dining room stretching to near 12 feet.

Looking to the rear of the house through the entrance hall, through the library and kitchen areas. The exquisite chandelier and stained glass windows adorn and typify the era of Victorian architecture.

16

The den is situated just behind the entrance hall, for many years the only downstairs bedroom. The warmth of the old Kelly house is reflected here and throughout this well-preserved and cared-for home. Patrick C. Kelly would very much approve of this portion of his legacy.

Retaining the style of the old does not require that today's guardians of history remain with all of the relics of the past. Bathrooms and kitchens can retain the flavor of the past while providing the comforts and conveniences of modern times. The original Kelly kitchen had a potbellied stove and, just behind, a coal-bin and laundry room.

The master bath.

One descendent remembers "many a night young and old would gather around the piano in the parlor for a song fest, that, on occasion, would see a passersby sitting on the curb outside enjoying the music." Here in the front parlor, and throughout the entire house, one gets the feeling of warm and toasty contentment that the Kelly legacy of comfort and good times of a hundred years past carries on into the future.

LESESNE HOUSE

The architectural style here is common to many homes built in the 19th-century South. There are two-storied, columned porches extending the length of a five-bay facade with a centrally located entrance surrounded with sidelights and transom.

One of Fernandina's few antebellum structures, this home was constructed circa 1860 for Dr. John F. Lesesne, a Fernandina physician. Built in a variant of Greek or Classical Revival architecture, its significant attributes are in its rectangular design, galleried porch, gabled roof, and its tall windows. The house was built of hand-hewn timbers and fastened with wooden pegs.

In 1868, just after the Civil War, the home was sold to Judge John Friend, a German immigrant who came to Fernandina from Ohio in 1865 as the newly appointed tax commissioner. He was later appointed county judge and was elected to the State Senate. Before taking the Senate seat, the Judge passed away. The house was inherited by the Judge's daughter Bertha who married Charles Angel. They passed the property to daughter Otilia Angel Starke, who in turn passed it to Angel Starke Davis. The last transfer of ownership was to the current family member, Marie Louise Davis Chaplin. This is a true, old family home.

The front sitting room is much like it has been for more than 100 years. In years past, floor-to-ceiling windows slid opened to cross ventilate rooms that today know heat pumps and air-conditioners. The home's guardian fancies year-round holiday decor and the company of little "Angels" keeping the family spirit alive. Family furniture heirlooms abound and old photographs decorate the walls.

The dining room of today's Lesesne House was at one time a porch that wrapped around from the front of the house. This was where the slaves and later the hired hands greeted and assisted the owners, who whisked them off to whatever chores needed to be accomplished. After Judge Friend purchased the house, he enclosed the porch for his law office.

The Lesesne House is cheerful year 'round with the spirit of Christmas and the decor befitting the antiquity of the 19th century. As with many of Fernandina's historic old homes, the floors and trim are original native yellow pine in magnificent condition.

LEWIS TABBY HOUSE

One of the most exceptional pieces of architecture on Amelia Island is the Tabby House, primarily due to the material used in its construction. Designed by Robert Schuyler and constructed from 1882 to 1885 for Charles W. Lewis, this home is unique to all of Amelia Island. It is the only structure on the island built during the late 19th century using tabby with poured portland cement. The irregularity of outline, use of the rounded arch, and elaborate balustrades add to the uniqueness of the structure.

Charles W. Lewis came to Amelia Island from Massachusetts in 1867 and operated a milling and merchandising business. He became the United States. Land Commissioner and later was the town postmaster.

For many years the Tabby House was also called the Mularkey House as it was the residence of John Mularkey and his family. John and his brother Daniel operated a large drygoods store at 210 Centre Street.

By the mid-20th century the house was abandoned and heavily vandalized. The house's saviors came in 1965 when the Wilson family purchased and lovingly restored the home to her 1880's condition. She was reroofed, rewired, and the crumbling plaster removed. By 1973, it was individually listed on the National Register of Historic Places.

SEVENTH STREET

A newspaper article dated October 3, 1885, entitled "A Handsome Residence" told of the home's completion.

"The walls are built entirely of concrete and Mr. Lewis has erected it in a very leisurely manner, giving the walls abundant time to harden and settle as they progressed, and has paid the utmost attention to every detail of construction, to secure comfort and healthfulness as well as stability. The exterior, cemented with the best of portland cement will be impervious to moisture, while all dampness from capillary attraction is cut off by an impervious course of cement composition beneath the first floor joist.

"The house is very irregular in outline, presenting two fronts facing the streets on which it is located. On 7th Street, it presents a semi-octagon, bayed front, and a recessed vestibule porch, with tiled floor - the principle entrance - the buttressed steps leading to which, when completed, will be of one solid block of artificial stone; and on Ash Street it shows a handsome bay window and a neat private entrance; and in the angle formed by the two sections of the building is an abundance of piazza to both stories. A very handsome roof crowned the edifice, with its irregular and broken skyline and relieved with dormer windows and ornamental chimney tops; upon the summit a spacious deck commands an extended and pleasing view.

"The interior is well arranged and convenient; the rooms are spacious, and present a pleasing variety of form. The principal rooms and stair hall of the first story are arranged *en suite*, with wide communications, and all open upon the piazza; and the details of domestic economy are not overlooked. The service stairs, butler's pantry, store-pantry, closets and kitchen offices, have received their share of attention, and are conveniently arranged with bathroom, presses, etc. A large and airy attic above insures cool and well-ventilated rooms below."

Brilliant colors were common to the Victorian period.

A close-up of the poured tabby wall at the 7th Street entrance.

Historic American Building Survey

The south wing of the Tabby house was Lewis' music room where today the home's guardian continues the tradition.

Looking from the exterior of the music room's bay window, the smooth walls and window dressings are contrasted with course concrete tabby, simple window hoods, and protective shutters.

LUCY COTTAGE

Lucy cottage is one of three side-by-side homes belonging to members of the Senator William Naylor Thompson, Jr. family. William Thompson was a native of Harper's Ferry, Virginia, and member of Florida's 7th Regiment, Confederate States of America, when wounded in 1864 at the Battle of Decatur, Georgia. Thompson was employed by the Florida Railroad Company in 1869 and rose to become the Treasurer of the Florida Central & Peninsular Railroad. By 1876, he was elected to the Florida legislature and was elected to the Florida Senate in 1892. He served there until his accidental death in 1896.

This two-story frame vernacular can be designated Gothic Revival with its steeply pitched gables and pointed arches. It was designed by John Hedges and constructed in 1872 at the beginning of Fernandina's golden era. It belonged to Lucy Thompson Haverstick, the Senator's sister.

The house survives as one of the community's many little diamonds. The cottage is noteworthy for its decorative vergeboards along the east and south gables, its steep roof, and false dormer. The Senator lived next door at 11 South 7th Street and his son lived on the opposite side of Lucy's cottage in what is believed to be the oldest brick home in new Fernandina.

The narrow, lancet windows are a tradition of Gothic architecture.

The large family and music room faces east, drawing in most of the morning sun. Restoration has retained its yellow pine floors, trim and period mantle.

The center of the house staircase.

MEDDAUGH HOUSE

The front entrance.

By 1895, the Meddaughs had moved on and by the turn of the century the house was occupied by a Joel Pilsbury and Howard Ravenel.

As with many large old homes of the 19th century, the early 20th century brought with it conversion to apartments. It now is a single-family, private residence.

The entrance hall and central staircase are in the original McGinnis section of the house.

This was the original residence of Joseph McGinnis, a Fernandina grocer, and is said to have been a single-story frame home and is believed to have been constructed in the mid-1850's. The Historic Properties Survey of Fernandina Beach lists the construction at 1872-1875, however, it is believed that date is when major changes were made to the house. McGinnis sold to Francis A. Meddaugh in 1875. The Meddaugh family had come to Fernandina in 1855 and are listed as grocers in the early 1870's.

Shortly after its purchase, Meddaugh expanded the house to its present size, which architecturally is considered a frame vernacular residence.

The 1886, the city directory indicates the owner as James E. Meddaugh, a grocer with a store at Centre and 3rd Streets. James Meddaugh was elected Tax Collector in Fernandina in 1882 and 1883. He served as High Sheriff of Nassau County circa 1880.

Convergence of the central, first-floor hallway, the dining room and front sitting parlors is the larger part of the original house. The cornice moldings, chair rails, and symmetrically milled door trim and decorative corner blocks were used in many homes of the post-Civil War period.

The front sitting room.

The dining parlor was at the rear of the original house but, with additions, is now centrally located.

One of the grand old homes of North 2nd Street.

MERROW HOUSE

This was originally the residence of Josiah H.P. Merrow, a lumberman who had served in the Union Army and fought in this location during the Civil War. He later returned from Maine to live, introducing his family to Fernandina.

The Merrow House sits on a bluff that was at one time simply called "The Hill." It is the highest point overlooking the harbor, but the bluff was, in effect, man-made. It overlooks harbor facilities that, as they developed, have flattened or removed the hill to within yards of the house.

The house's third-story tower windows are high enough that the tall-masted lumber schooners and barges could be seen as they navigated the channel between Cumberland and Amelia Islands and made their way south to the harbor.

Josiah Merrow's son, Samuel, is said to have lived in the house as late as 1950. The house remained vacant for many years until the mid-1980's when redevelopment of the Port of Fernandina by its overseers, the Ocean Highway and Port Authority (OHPA), changed the home's fate.

The OHPA contracted with locally owned Nassau Terminals, in 1986, managing the port until 1990, when the company was purchased by the Rotterdam based terminal operator, Van Ommeren. Continuing to operate as Nassau Terminals, Inc., the company invested heavily in the restoration of Josiah's old home under the guidance of Bill Kavanaugh, one of the original owners of Nassau Terminals. Kavanaugh and Nassau Terminals, Inc., recognized the potential of the old house as port management offices due to its location on the hill. They also realized that, when restored, they will have made a magnificent contribution to the historic integrity of their community.

The two-story frame vernacular residential home is noteworthy for its two-story galleried porches, arched glass windows in the front doors, and the large transom window over the front door.

The home now houses the office of Nassau Terminals, the managers and operators of the Port of Fernandina.

The sitting room hearth.

The original heart-pine floors remain an essential element of the historic structure though carpeting covers it in several offices. Wainscoting and chair rails surround each room, and fireplaces, though inactivated, adorn a corner of each room.

The Merrow house second-floor bedrooms have been converted to office space, preserving the pine floors and spectacular views up and down the Amelia River. The narrow staircase to the cupola remains, now used only occasionally by the company curious.

Downstairs newel post.

The view from the cupola is south to the Rayonier plant, along the river's edge to Old Town and Cumberland Sound.

Collection of David & Iris Jacobson

Circa 1920.

MOUNT HOPE
PLANTATION

ALSO KNOWN AS
THE OLD NEST & BUENA VISTA

Vegetation on the grounds of today's Mount Hope Plantation are a variety of oak, pecan, hickory, palm, persimmon, pear, and plum. Obvious to the eye are a number of mature grafted trees, pecans atop of hickory, believed to have been joined in the 1940's for disease resistance and the hickory's larger root structure. These trees today produce an abundance of pecans with an occasional hickory nut. Directly in front of the house is a camphor tree (the large tree in the photo above) that was damaged by fire when Union troops burned the original structure in 1862.

Amelia Island's Mount Hope Plantation is an awe-inspiring lesson in restoration and preservation. In 1797, a Spanish land grant awarded John D. Vaughan 250 acres near the midpoint of Amelia Island between the South Amelia River and the Atlantic Ocean. The original plantation house was built within the year by Vaughan, at first known as The Old Nest and later as Buena Vista. Vaughan was a Revolutionary War officer who is believed to have fought with George Washington at Valley Forge. His plantation house was burned by occupying Union forces in 1862, but reconstructed the same year. The plantation house remained in the Vaughan family for 150 years and is now in just its third ownership.

As with so many other structures along the tidewaters of Amelia, the current owners have meticulously and lovingly patched the past to the present. Here a decaying relic was rescued from destruction, stripped of 100 years of remodeling, cleaned, polished, and reassembled to its historical greatness, its fate having nearly succumbed to high-rise development.

On the ground level is a sitting parlor and dining room, divided by a narrow hallway and the stairway to the second floor. Above are two bedrooms and another dividing hallway. Verandas the full width of the house, typical of Georgian architecture, are on both levels of the front and rear of the house.

The carriage house, patio, and two-story veranda that allows one a magnificent view of the South Amelia River area (below).

In restoration, a large family living area was added to the north end. The original kitchen was modernized, and a breezeway built connecting to the old carriage house at the home's northwest side. Patios were laid and the driveway was paved. It took two-and-a-half years to restore and add to the old home that is now one of a small number of Georgian style plantation homes in Florida. Many non-period architectural changes made in the previous 75 years have been reversed.

The house today has been restored to 1862 architecture, without gingerbread, crown molding or many of the niceties that may have gone into it had the war not had such an impact. Owners then, even large landowners, had little money or inclination to go beyond necessities of food, shelter, and safety of their families.

For nearly 175 years a road or path ran from the front of the old plantation house, northeast to the shore of the ocean, obstructed only in recent years by oceanfront development. Slave quarters were scattered along what today is referred to as Scott Road. Family sources note the slave count at the plantation was as high as 500; census records note considerably less.

Looking southwest from the old plantation house, across the marshes toward the South Amelia River and beyond, the Nassau River.

Restoration of the 1862 home has slightly widened the hallway dividing the dining (left) and living room areas. The banister and staircase are tooled of cypress with original wainscot parallel to the floor and along the staircase to the second floor.

Restoration has returned fireplaces to Civil War era tradition. Modifications made half a century ago added rooms on the back side of this dining room, sealed the front of the dining room fireplace, and opened it in the new room addition. In the recent restoration the process was reversed, relocating the fireplace opening to its original location. An antique mantle was purchased that closely matches the living room hearth. Old marble slabs found on the grounds, believed to have been from old sinks or counter tops, were cut, polished, and now frame the hearth. Only the firebricks are new, installed to meet current codes. The pine flooring is from the 1862 house, restored to original beauty.

The 1797 fireplace had been covered many years ago with a more modern yellow brick. Renovations uncovered the original wooden facade crafted in the Civil War period which was then restored to its original finish. The old brick and mortar were removed, cleaned, and reset in the original location of the 1797 home.

An exceptionally comfortable family room added on the north side of the original old home.

The spacious kitchen area adjoining the family room was added some 40 years ago and updated with the recent restoration and additions to the old house.

JOHN PALMER HOUSE

Dr. John Denham Palmer was a medical doctor fresh out of the University of Maryland School of Medicine when he came to Amelia Island. The year was 1872. He was from one of Florida's pioneer medical families, born in 1850 at Monticello, the son of Dr. Thomas and Jane Palmer. He located on Amelia Island in a period when it was becoming one of Florida's most important cities. The young Dr. Palmer established a practice and began to build a formidable reputation.

The year 1877 came and so too did yellow fever. It was late summer when the Jacksonville Board of Health sent a physician to inspect the situation with Fernandina's Health Officer, Dr. B.B. Pope. Joined with Dr. Palmer, the three found 25 cases of the dreaded fever, mostly in the area of low, swampy land. By mid-September it reached epidemic proportions. Dr. Palmer work tirelessly, rendering aid and comfort, and he came down with a case of the fever from which he fortunately was able to recover. In Memphis, in 1878, when that city experienced a similar epidemic, the doctor donated his experience and skills toward the recovery of that city. The City of Memphis awarded him with a medal in recognition for his contributions to the health care of its citizens.

Dr. Palmer returned to Fernandina and his family where he again fought the ravages of the fever in the 1880's. Dr. Palmer and his wife found property along Atlantic Avenue, then nothing more than a trail through the forest en route to the beach and the lighthouse. He purchased the land, contracted with William and John Mann, and began the building process. The year was 1891.

Dr. Palmer and his wife lived in the house until 1905. His practice was operated out of his home during much of their life there. For many years he owned and operated Palmer Brother Drugs with his brother on Centre Street.

At the age of 55, John and his wife moved to Jacksonville where he passed away on November 3, 1912. In 1931, the house was rented to the Ernest Davis family of Crandall who stayed in the Palmer house for about a year. By 1948, Joseph M. Oxley purchased and relocated his Oxley Funeral Home business from downtown Fernandina to the Palmer house, later becoming Oxley Mortuary, Inc. In 1974, the firm was purchased by Jack Heard, who by the 1980's,

A now highly modified carriage house sits behind the main house where it has been for 110 years.

renamed the business Oxley-Heard Funeral Directors.

The John Denham Palmer House is a massive two-and-a-half story structure of great prominence along Atlantic Avenue. It is sometimes overlooked as an important part of the historic community because of its distance from the heart of downtown Fernandina.

The most prominent features are its two-story galleried porch extending the entire width of the facade and a portion of the east side, and its hipped and gabled roof. Four chimneys and eight fireplaces adorn the massive structure. The front door opens into a central hallway with the main staircase running north and parlors to each side. These were the sitting and dining areas. Each of the rooms are separated with large pocket doors.

The Palmer House exhibits a higher level of vernacular tradition in Fernandina showing the influences of the Colonial Revival style.

Original light fixtures installed about 1920 when electricity came to Atlantic Avenue.

Half of the second floor today houses an apartment while the other is meeting and storage rooms. These were the bedrooms from the days when the Palmer house was a private residence. All of the mantles are crafted of yellow pine and located in the corner of the room nearest the center of the house. They share flues with fireplaces directly below on the first floor.

Similar to those of the second floor, four first floor hearths are near the center of the house on either side of the main dividing hallway.

Carpet now covers the two-inch thick heart-pine floors for safety and noise reduction. Each of the home's two staircases have ornamented newels with the front staircase shown here having chamfered balusters.

Rooms are spacious, reflecting the size of the home. Ten foot high pocket doors are heavy and hard to slide, but still function to provide spacious living areas or, as it is today, ample room for guests attending viewings or funeral services of any size.

PHELAN - VEROT HOUSE

Little more than a block off of Centre Street, this 1865 restored cottage survives as an major chapter of Amelia Island history.

It was the year that the War Between The States ended, 1865, when construction began on a small cottage at 116 North 4th Street. Its owners were William and Sarah Phelan about whom little is known today. They lived in the house until 1876 when William presumably died and Sarah sold her home for $900 to Bishop Jean-Pierre Augustin Verot, Apostolic Vicar of Florida from St. Augustine. The Bishop was concerned over the living conditions of the nuns serving St. Michael's Parish.

In 1871, two nuns, Sisters Celini and Helen, had come to Fernandina from a school and convent of the Sisters of St. Joseph in Jacksonville. Their mission was to prepare children of St. Michael's for their first Holy Communion. They moved from a rented house at Broome and 8th Streets to the Verot house. They were joined by four more sisters and Sister Celini became the Mother Superior. Within a year of moving to their new cottage, two great tragedies would occur.

In 1876, the first great fire of Fernandina devastated the city from the docks to 3rd Street, a point just a block away from their new home. In 1877, yellow fever spread across the island with more than 1,100 of the 1,600 inhabitants eventually contracting the disease. The Sisters worked night and day nursing victims here in their own home and around the city, earning themselves the name, "Angels of Mercy." Mother Celini and Sister deSales fell victims of the dreaded disease and were buried in the church yard. They were later buried in Bosque Bello Cemetery.

The Sisters of St. Joseph lived in the home until 1882 when a formal convent was completed. The house passed into private ownership and eventually to disrepair. It would be 1990 before being restored to its original beauty and usefulness. Today it is a prized, private residence. This vernacular residential structure labeled Folk Victorian is noteworthy for its transom window over the door, jigsaw cut brackets, and chamfered porch posts.

The front parlor retains the pine floors and a flair of 19th-century Victorian wallpaper so popular in the period.

Peering from the master bedroom, across the stairwell, to a second bedroom and bath facilities. Door and window trim are simple reflecting a time at Civil War's end when supplies were few and fancy was not a priority.

On the second floor are found pine floors that required massive repairs in the restoration, marginal but understandably low headroom, and walls and ceilings finished everywhere with tongue and groove timbers. Windows on either end of the gable roof design and two gabled dormers on the street side provide ample light and ventilation to this quaint cottage of old.

The front entry is into a hall that splits the parlor from the dining room, typical of 19th- and early 20th-century homes of various architectural styles. The open doorway on the far right of the photograph leads to the kitchen that at one time occupied a separate building to the rear.

GIDEON PALMER HOUSE

The arcaded front veranda.

An 1890's image shows James Smythe and Lottie Winifred Elledge at the horse; at the fence corner Bernice and her father Houston Elledge; on the porch is James Smythe's parents and another unidentified couple. Second from the left on the second floor porch is Florence Blanchard; the others are not identified.

Late in December of 1886, Gideon Palmer of Middlesex County, Connecticut purchased the north half of lot number 1 of block number 128 from the Florida Town Improvement Company at a cost of $500. Two years later, construction at 302 South 7th Street was completed by builder Frederick W. Plumb.

Title of the home passed to Eliza W. Palmer, Gideon's wife, to Charlotte M. Palmer, then to Julia and Thomas J. Streety (perhaps the mortgage holder) who paid $3200, all prior to 1895. Houston Elledge was the next owner, residing there through the turn of the century. Elledge was a conductor on the Florida Central & Peninsular Railroad out of Fernandina, as was his son-in-law and next door neighbor, Edwin A. Blanchard.

Two early weddings that occurred in the house were James Smythe to Lottie Elledge on December 27, 1892 and Ed Blanchard to Florence Elledge on July 26, 1896.

By 1907, Sally R. Mahoney purchased the house, retaining it in her family for generations. Like other spacious homes dating to the 19th century, the Gideon Palmer house was converted to an apartment house through the rough years of the depression.

The vernacular architectural style Gideon Palmer house is a

Two of the most outstanding architectural attributes are its gables and shingled siding.

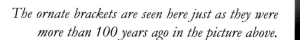

The ornate brackets are seen here just as they were more than 100 years ago in the picture above.

The front sitting parlor.

The central hall.

magnificent prize of South 7th Street, steeped in Gothic Revival with Italianate influences. Its ornate brackets below the soffit encircle the entire rectangular structure; staggered shingles surround the second floor, all today painted in authentic period color.

The interior displays beautifully restored yellow pine floors, trim, and wainscotting along the central hall walls.

The second-floor rear bedroom is a child's hideaway just as it was more than 100 years ago when Alva Guy Blanchard was born in this room to parents Florence and Edwin Blanchard.

The master bedroom and bath suite retains its 19th-century charm, even as the restoration of door casings and trim continue.

Porches of the Prescott House's first and second level have railing designs of Chippendale influence, carved bracketing above, chamfered columns, and a two-story ornately decorated bay window.

The shutters frame, protect, and beautify the entrance door capped with a clear-glass transom.

PRESCOTT HOUSE

Josiah Prescott was one of the many Union soldiers that returned to Fernandina after the Civil War to make this his new home. He was a lieutenant of the local occupation forces. Prescott purchased the property at 120 North 6th Street in 1872 and completed construction of the original structure in 1876.

Architecturally Prescott's home is frame vernacular with Queen Anne influence in its bay windows, ornamented brackets, and spacious rooms of various sizes and shapes.

Prescott also built a two-story commercial establishment on the northwest corner of Centre and 2nd Streets and there operated a shoe store and haberdashery until the turn into the twentieth century. It was then sold and was converted into the Palace Saloon.

The porch on the north side of the house provides shade and a relaxed atmosphere for its owners.

The original Prescott house included two rooms on each floor with a spacious hall and staircase connecting the two on the south side of the house. To the rear was a separate kitchen most likely connected with a breezeway.

Major additions were made on the back of the house in the 1890's that included a dining room and kitchen on the first floor and a parlor, a third bedroom, and a bathroom on the second floor.

In the 1920's, another addition was added to the 1890's section providing a pantry, half-bath, and rear stairway leading to two additional bedrooms in the rear. The wall separating those two bedrooms was removed in recent years to facilitate a large master bedroom with a now freestanding hearth where the wall had been. A garage was built with the 1920's and was lengthened in later years to accommodate larger cars. The original drive circled the house, but, as a misplaced cedar tree grew on the south side, the narrow drive became impassable and is no longer usable.

Ernest Davis of Crandall purchased the house in 1932 from a Prescott daughter for $2500, primarily to ease his children's progression into high school at Fernandina. The Davis children, Ernest, Jr., Stewart, Kathleen, and Suzanne, lived their young-adult lives in this house. Ernest, Sr., passed in 1946 and by 1952 the house was sold by his widow to the Doherty family. Years later, they sold the property to the Libby family.

Strong architectural attributes of the Prescott house are in its first-floor ornamented veranda, its Chinese Chippendale balustrades, bracketed cornices, and two-story bay windows.

The second room of the first floor is today an entertainment area that connects the original house with the kitchen and other additions of the last 100 years.

A traditional staircase with beautifully doweled balusters connect Prescott's two original first-floor rooms with the bedroom suites above.

At the rear of the second floor were several small rooms designed as living spaces for live-in help. With restoration and modifications to the old home, several walls were removed providing one large master bedroom that retains the fireplace and small staircase down to the kitchen area.

Sawed brackets surround the house below the eaves.

The front sitting room exhibits the original heart pine flooring and pine trim.

Detail of the sitting room hearth

RUTISHAUSER HOUSE
ALSO KNOWN AS
THE STEAMBOAT HOUSE

Viewing the Steamboat house is like strolling back a 130 years, gazing at a massive array of spindles, brackets, and balusters.

The veranda is reminiscent of 19th century Mississippi steamboat-style architecture.

This beautiful example of Mississippi steamboat architecture was constructed in 1883 for Edward L. Bill, a native of Wheeling, West Virginia. The frame vernacular structure is somewhat unique to any other design in the historic district. It is best remembered as the home of J. J. Rutishauser who operated a drinking establishment on lower Ash Street. Mr. Rutishauser was the first Assistant Fire Chief in 1900. Still on the property is Rutishauser's roadside stepping stone that once assisted gents and their ladies into their coaches.

The exterior is noteworthy for its turned and spindlework ornamentation on the two-story veranda, cross-gabling, and for the two-story octagonal bay windows.

The initials of Mr. Rutishauser (J. J. R.) identified the stone and home as originally belonging to one of Fernandina's early pub owners. Time has taken its toll in a small chip pierced from a corner of the old monument.

40

The sitting parlor with a tin ceiling, somewhat unique in residential construction.

Painted white throughout, the interior trim and molding is yellow pine as is true with most homes of the community. Floors are yellow pine and the ceilings are a towering 11 feet in height. Total square footage is 2860 with approximately 1000 feet of wrapping veranda. The house is noteworthy for its turned and spindle-work ornamentation on the two-story veranda, cross gables, and for its two-story octagonal window facing 10th Street.

From the staircase landing to the front room.

The entry hall, staircase, and tin ceiling remain very much as they were when the home was constructed in 1883.

Partially hidden amongst the hardwood trees at 214 South 7th Street is a comfortable home built in 1889 by Samuel A. Swann for his son Donovan. Samuel Swann was a railroad official and head of the Fernandina Town Development Company. The house sold in 1900 and went through several owners by 1907 when it and an adjacent lot were purchased by D. A. Kelly for $3,500.

Kelly owned and operated a ship's chandlery at the old Hoyt Building at the corner of Centre and North 2nd Streets. Kelly served in the Florida Legislature and was one of the community's most outstanding civic leaders.

Architecturally, the home is best described as shingle-style Queen Anne. Its tower, spacious veranda, second-level porch, and assortment of stained-glass windows that climb along the interior staircase are the home's most noteworthy features. Dark-stained yellow pine lavishly blankets the interior. The entrance hall is cloaked with deeply-stained pine that runs up the staircase, along the walls, around the trim, and across the ceiling. It embodies an imposingly Victorian mood.

The three fireplaces on the first floor, all in separate rooms, join to make use of a single flue. Fireplaces on the second floor also tap into the same chimney. This was common in homes of the wealthy as well as the less expensive vernacular designs.

The house received major restoration work in 1975 and now displays itself as a marvelous piece of Fernandina's Victorian era.

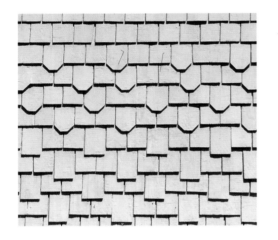

Shingles of varying shapes adorn the entire second level adding unique character.

The entrance hall with its extensive display of dark-stained yellow pine.

SWANN / KELLY HOUSE

The front sitting parlor features windows at the base of
the tower and a warmth of Victoria.

A relic of the original furnishings is still in use at the
head of the staircase - a simple weight-lifting device capped
with iron ornamentation. Along the north wall of the
stairway are beautiful stained-glass windows original to the
house of the 1880's.

The dining parlor as seen from the front sitting room, past the
large sliding doors to a table awaiting its guests.

The original pre-Civil War house faced Date Street, seen here in the center and left, blending magnificently into the massive turn-into-the-20th-century addition facing South 7th Street.

WAAS HOUSE

WAAS HOUSE

The high mantle of the entrance hall.

Dr. William Theodore Waas

One can envision the good Doctor Waas' buggy as its horse trots down South 7th Street, returning home for dinner from his drugstore on Centre Street, possibly having stopped to chat with his friend Effingham Bailey along the way. Approaching his home, his two young daughters dressed in white lace are skating around the veranda, a steady plum of smoke is rising from the kitchen chimney, and the aroma of apple pie is drifting from the area of open kitchen windows. Little Kate and sister Theo were about to be given a good talking to, knowing their father didn't allow skating on the porch.

The entrance hall staircase, with its spindled artistry, is the focal point of William T. Wass' 1900 addition.

Previous page: The exterior of the Waas house features the spacious wrapping veranda with its corner gazebos, a three-story tower, sidelights and transom at the main entrance, bracketing, decorative spindles, stick-style trusses, and fishscale shingles.

The initial construction of this magnificent house was in 1856 and 1857, originally the residence of the Hedges family in that pre-Civil War time period. It was much smaller and simpler for half a century, essentially that portion of what is seen today facing Date Street (insert on previous page). After the Hedges sold, it went through several owners including St. Peters Episcopal Church.

The Queen Anne style residence is known today as the Waas House as it sits majestically at the corner of Date and South 7th Streets, a private residence as it has always been.

By 1899, the house was purchased by Dr. William T. Waas, born and reared in Fernandina the son of John and Regina Waas. The doctor and his wife immediately began renovating and enlarging, changing its outward appearance to the then elegant Queen Anne style, adding a bit of Gothic Revival. The home was given a vastly larger interior and the family living area was relocated to the new wing. A new main entrance was constructed facing South 7th Street.

As a young man, William had attended school in Fernandina, then went off to the East Florida Seminary at Gainesville. He graduated from the Tulane Medical School before returning to Fernandina where he associated himself with Dr. J. D. Palmer. With Palmer's death, Dr. Waas bought the Palmer Pharmacy and operated it at Centre and 4th

The Waas taste for elegance is apparent in the art surrounding their 7th Street entrance.

The warmth of terra-cotta is seen in the hearths of the entrance hall and the dining parlor, adding earth tones to the charm of this Victorian pearl. Terra-cotta is a high grade of weathered or aged clay which, when mixed with sand or pulverized fired clay, can be molded and fired at high temperatures to a hardness not attainable with brick. The word terra-cotta is Latin for "cooked earth."

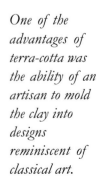

One of the advantages of terra-cotta was the ability of an artisan to mold the clay into designs reminiscent of classical art.

An office for the current guardians was at one time the front parlor of the Waas family. Above the bay window, and at the right in the dining room, are spandrels, typically used to define an entryway or to separate one room area from another. These gingerbread creations added a touch of opulent detail to rooms already alive with colors and detail.

The dining room is where daughter Kate Waas Clogg remembers Christmas the best, and the big trees her father brought home and decorated with candles, long before commercial Christmas bulbs were available.

Streets for many years as the Waas Drug Store. He practiced medicine from an office within his home and, as a public-spirited man, held positions with both the City of Fernandina and Nassau County.

The tower niche with a decorative spandrel delineating the little sitting area from the dining parlor.

Kate Waas and older sister Theo's bedroom was just above the new entrance on South 7th Street. There was a small porch where the girls could play with their dolls and talk to their friends out on the sidewalk. The master bedroom was over the dining room, both being a part of the tower at the north end of the house. Behind their bedroom was the only indoor bathroom in the entire house.

Having lived a long and fruitful life, including being the Mayor of Fernandina from 1899 to 1908, the doctor died at his home on April 25, 1936. Dozier Waas continued to live in the house with her sister. During the 1940 war years, she gave the house to her daughter, Kate, who with her husband cared for the two elderly sisters until their passing. In 1952, Kate sold the house to her nephew, Glyn Waas, and in doing so kept the beautiful home in the family.

The Waas Drug Store was carried on by William's son, Glyndon H. Waas, and later his son, Glyndon "Glyn" H. Waas, Jr., before being sold out of the family in the late 1990's.

"The pocket doors to the dining room were closed the
night before Christmas," recalled Kate. "It was always cold
in the house, having only fireplaces for heat."

A peek from the entrance hall is a marvelous tribute to those that lived their lives here so many years ago.

VILLA LAS PALMAS

Villa Las Palmas is one of the gems of historic Fernandina. The Villa Las Palmas architectural design is eclectic in that it shows primary signatures of Mediterranean Revival, yet boasts Art Nouveau, Colonial Revival, and shingle styles. The villa is most noteworthy for its broad three-sided veranda and spacious living area within.

Villa Las Palmas was built for prosperous, 52-year-old Nathaniel B. Borden from 1905 to 1910, a gift to his 17-year-old bride, Florence "Flossie" Reynard of Brooklyn, New York. In the building of Villa Las Palmas, John R. Mann was the contractor who, at the instruction of Borden,

built a warm and comfortable home in massive proportions of cedar shingles, masonry columns, numerous arches, and capped with a widow's-walk perch.

The Bordens were frequent entertainers and so the rooms were designed for guest flow.

Borden was then the Cuban Consul, a lumber exporter, and highly respected entrepreneur. He later also became the Norwegian consul and held both positions for many years.

Before coming to Fernandina, Borden was employed by William D. Wheelwright & Co., a New York lumber company, from 1878 to circa 1890. He learned the trade in detail and attained the position of managing partner. He resigned his position and established himself jobbing and exporting lumber. The shipping business expanded with his company becoming the largest enterprise of its kind in Fernandina. Borden operated his own ships and docking facilities and sold yellow pine and cypress around the world.

Borden's most highly publicized activities surrounded his involvement in what was known as the Fernandina Filibuster and covert activities smuggling arms into Cuba in the mid-1890's. His client, who he repre-

The late afternoon sun spills through the clear glass of the magnificent entry and into the front sitting room.

The spacious entry hall and staircase area glisten with natural light from the south through an abundance of glass pains in the door, broad sidelights, and the Palladian window above. Though not original to the house, the brass chandelier adapts itself elegantly to its period surroundings.

The three-level circular staircase winds its way to the widows walk at the peak of the roof. The staircase, as with all of the house trim, is of heart pine, then easily obtainable from forests of interior Nassau County.

sented, was the Cuban freedom fighter Jose Marti.

A large cash of arms was discovered by U.S. government agents in Borden's warehouse on the docks of Fernandina, making headlines in New York papers. Borden was questioned but released since his efforts failed. However, the incident gave Jose Marti's cause a great boost. Years later, the president of Cuba bestowed the honorary rank of colonel upon Borden for his wartime efforts.

During his lifetime here, Borden served on the city council, was elected Mayor of Fernandina in 1910, and was a director of the Citizens National Bank. In his later life, Colonel Borden lost most of his fortune in the depression. He died in 1938 at the age of 76.

Mrs. Borden lived in the villa until 1944, with the remainder of her life at Fernandina's Keystone Hotel and with her son in Washington, D.C., where she died. Villa Las Palmas sold in 1944 to local shrimping pioneer Harry Sahlman for $12,000.

Windows surround the first-floor rooms affording its owners a maximum of airflow in the summer months and ample sunshine from the south.

The music room is on the first floor and was designed spaciously for entertaining and comfortable living. Walls, trim, and flooring are much as they were when Nathaniel Borden and his bride first stepped through the front door. The original mantle is ornate with ceramic tiles. The original chandeliers were sold with most of Borden's trappings in 1944.

The view from Borden's music room (now the living room), through the entry hall, to the parlor still invites gala holiday socials. Guest flow was an obvious benefit of Borden's 12,000 square foot villa.

Shutters disperse the rays of the afternoon sun and cool the music room and parlor. Wall-to-wall carpeting was removed by the current owners, revealing the original pine floors installed shortly after the turn of the 20th century. Beautiful area rugs now protect Borden's dark-stained pine flooring.

The parlor (above) is an extension of the music room and entry hall that together have seen social and music gatherings for almost 100 years. The broad pocket doors rarely close to separate Borden's unusually large floor plan.

HISTORIC INNS

FROM TREASURES OF THE PAST

What better way to promote restoration and preservation than to display these architectural treasures of the past as bed and breakfasts of the present. Pride and deep personal commitment is the engine that runs innkeepers in their ventures that require them to be gardeners, housekeepers, cooks, plumbers, waiters, bookkeepers, and gracious hosts. It is in their best interests that they maintain the highest of preservation standards that, in-turn, sell their product, guest accommodations in a Victorian era atmosphere.

Seldom will one find out-of-era architecture at any of the inns of historic Amelia Island. Architecturally, building exteriors are regulated by historic district codes. The depth of interior era architecture is at the discretion of the innkeeper. Most of the inns photographed within this work maintain era tradition adapted to guest comfort.

The history of Amelia's historic homes that were turned into bed and breakfasts varies according to the affluence of their original owners. Several are monumental in appearance, while others reflect a modest size, yet articulate artistic creativity of designers and builders. All maintain the Old Southern charm and character that built this little seaport more than 150 years ago.

614 Ash Street

ADDISON HOUSE

Historically the Simmons House

This balloon frame edifice of the Victorian era was built in 1876, the year of the great fire of Fernandina, yet one of the early years of the community's golden era.

The two-story structure's beginnings are somewhat sketchy, however, tradition has it that she was used as an infirmary during the yellow fever epidemics of the 1870's and 1880's. Speculation is that this was one of the Roux family houses, a name that had come to the island early on.

During the 1890's and at the turn of the century, the house was owned by a Frank Simmons, a Centre Street news dealer and stationer. He, too, was a partner with his neighbor, Effingham Bailey, in the streetcar business. The partners elected to run the tracks along Centre Street, down South 7th to Beech Street, and east to the ball park.

After the turn of the century, the house passed into the D. H. Grounds family. Mr. Grounds was the Superintendent of the Seaboard Railroad.

The interior has seen several renovations, one in the 1970's that converted the house into apartments and the major restoration in 1991, when the home was converted to a bed and breakfast. Sold in 1996, major additions were added to the side and rear, architecturally in tune with the 1870's original structure.

The Addison House takes it name from the daughter of the first bed-and-breakfast innkeepers.

The west and south walls of the old home are now joined by three recent additions in support of the home's bed and breakfast role. The entrance staircase (below) was once a part of the 19th-century Egmont Hotel located just down the street until razed more than a hundred years ago. The front doors, glass, and moldings are all original to the 1876 structure.

A view from the entrance.

The upper hallway.

The ceiling throughout the original house is 11 feet in height. The plaster ceiling medallion, heart pine floors, and heavy cornice are original to the house.

The spacious dining room.

AMELIA HOUSE

HISTORICALLY KNOWN AS THE LIBERTY BILLINGS HOUSE AND LATER THE LOTSPEICH HOUSE

The Amelia house sits quietly amongst ancient oaks and the oldest magnolia tree on the island, wrapped with an ancient wisteria vine.

The front parlor is cozy with fireplace and ornate with marbleized mantle, a technique the Victorian era favored.

Victorian-era designers put a lot of emphasis on wall coverings and only slightly less attention to ceilings. Since 1840, when the British invented a machine that made paper in continuous rolls, wallpaper became the preferred treatment of the middle class, finally able to afford wallpapers that substituted for panels, cornices, frieze molding, and columns.

The Amelia House is believed built by Liberty Billings, a former Colonel of the Union Army. Though its exact construction date is unknown, it is believed to have been built shortly after the Civil War, or about 1866-67.

Liberty Billings had been a chaplain in the 4th New Hampshire Infantry and an officer of the 33rd U.S. Colored troops. Assigned to Fort Clinch for most of the war, he returned at the war's conclusion with his wife, Lucinda. She died in 1869, with Liberty remarrying an Angela Osgood by 1876. Billings was a champion of Negro rights becoming a leader in the radical Republican movement of Florida's reconstruction. In 1870, he conducted the Nassau County census and was elected to the Florida Senate in 1871, representing Nassau, Duval, and St. Johns Counties until his death in the 1877.

The Amelia House's steeply gabled roof has an elaborate vergeboard and balustered porch with the exterior painted multiple colors to highlight its ornamentation. The interior ceilings are ten-and-a-half feet tall and the floors are original heart pine. The Lotspeich family purchased the house in the early 20th century and by the 1930's, converted it to an apartment. In 1990, the house was restored as a bed and breakfast, embellished with spandrels, crown moldings, and decorative carvings, the dining room and parlors masterfully decorated with Victorian era wallpaper on both walls and ceiling.

ASH STREET INN

A private residence for many years, the house was restored and is now maintained as a bed and breakfast inn.

The land on which the Ash Street Inn is located was at one time a part of the Domingo Fernandez Spanish Land Grant more than 200 years ago, as were all of the properties of today's Fernandina historic district. In succession, this corner property was purchased by the firm of Bellechasse & Finegan, the Florida Railroad Company, Joseph Finegan, the Florida Town Improvement Co., the Trustees of the Young Benevolent Branch Society, James Bell, Fred Hoyt, and again James Bell. All of the transfers of the property occurred prior to 1902 and each of the caretakers were well known in Amelia Island history.

In the 1890's, public records indicate that a building was located on the site. A mortgage on the property written in 1894 states that it covered "fixtures of the bakery." That would tell us the nature of the business that was there.

The present home was constructed in 1904 as a private residence for a Fernandina grocer. It was later purchased by a physician and used as his home and medical office. In what is today the first-floor bedroom, the good doctor brought many of the community's newborns into this world.

The house continued on as a private residence for many years. Floyd Wright owned the house until 1918 followed by the Hartwell family being its guardian until 1940. By the early 1990's, the house was purchased and converted into a bed and breakfast by the Waln family who operated it as the Walnford Inn until 2001, when it was again sold and shortly thereafter renamed the Ash Street Inn.

The entrance hall branches off to the front sitting parlor to the left, with an entryway fitted with the original pocket doors and brass fittings. Down the central hall is a first-floor sleeping room and beyond, the kitchen area. To the right is a sitting room believed to have been the original dining area.

The front parlor is now the dining area where the turn-of-the-century oak hearth remains.

The second floor landing at the front of the house connected the large single bedroom above with the rest of the sleeping quarters. Beautifully stained pine flooring and railings accentuate painted balusters and door and window moldings.

,Collection of S. Courtney McCranie

Circa 1905.

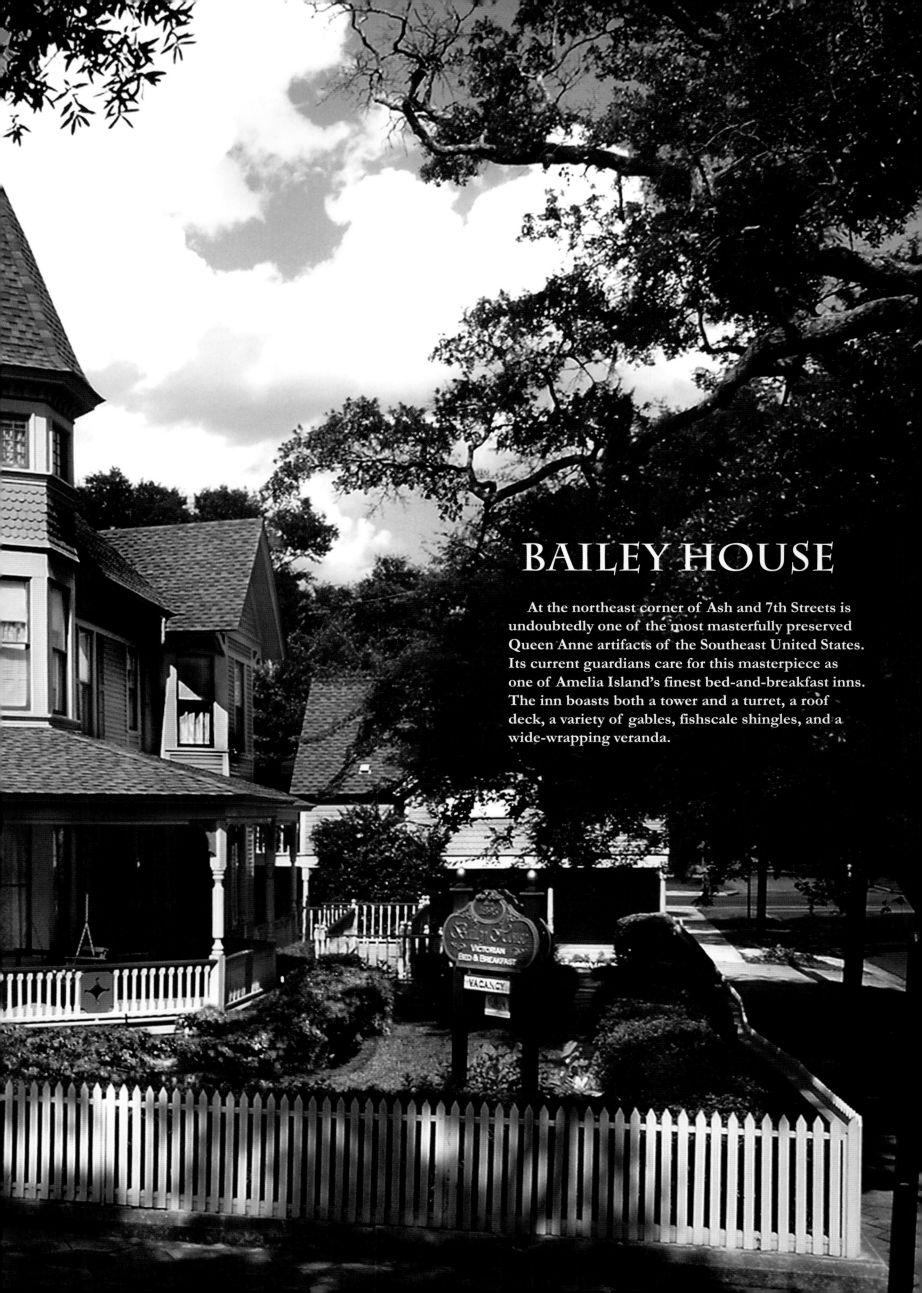

BAILEY HOUSE

At the northeast corner of Ash and 7th Streets is undoubtedly one of the most masterfully preserved Queen Anne artifacts of the Southeast United States. Its current guardians care for this masterpiece as one of Amelia Island's finest bed-and-breakfast inns. The inn boasts both a tower and a turret, a roof deck, a variety of gables, fishscale shingles, and a wide-wrapping veranda.

THE BAILEY HOUSE

To all who approach the many old homes of tidewater Amelia, there is an aura of time standing still, of great-grandma's house in Old Town, of carefree happy times as a child. The Bailey House is the epitome of that historical ambience from its imposing exterior to its interior charm. This is one of the most photographed Victorian homes of the South.

Effingham W. Bailey was the local agent for the Mallory Steamship Company and he was an entrepreneur of stature, with interests in lumber and phosphate. One of his business ventures included part ownership in the streetcar line that bounced along Centre, turned down South 7th Street, and ventured east all the way down Beech Street to the ocean.

Effingham wooed and won the heart of a beautiful young Kate MacDonell who lived with

A baby carriage found amongst relics in the attic was restored and now lends a bit of child's play to the staircase landing.

The reception hall, known simply as "the hearth hall," is warm and cozy with a brisk fire and memories that go back more than a hundred years. The mantel inscription "Hearth Hall - Welcome All" reflects the family's warmth. The old family Bible is always within reach. The Victrola in the corner at the far right is where it was sitting when the Baileys owned the house.

her parents in a comfortable home at 26 South 7th Street. That home was dismantled and the empty lot became a part of Bailey House property. Miss Kate was the daughter of Augustus O. MacDonell, resident manager of the Florida Railroad, and granddaughter of Alexander Harrison MacDonell, born on Amelia Island in 1809. His family owned and operated the Harrison Plantation south on Amelia Island.

A wedding gift from Kate's parents was the property adjacent to theirs, on the northeast corner of South 7th and Ash Streets. Effingham gave his new bride the choice of an elegantly constructed home with meager furnishings or a moderately priced house with tasteful and fine furnishings. She chose the former knowing the furnishings could be enhanced later.

The couple consulted a house plan book and chose a classic Victorian Queen Anne design by architect George W. Barber and Associates of Knoxville, Tennessee. Construction began in 1892, and, as with many of the finer homes of the community, ships, carpenters and boat builders masterfully crafted the woodwork. It was completed by 1895 at a cost of $10,000. Floors and trim were of clear bright yellow pine from local forests, Tiffany-style windows adorned the entrance hall, ceilings were high, six fireplaces warmed rooms and halls, and pocket doors opened to grandeur and graciousness.

Its Queen Anne design is ornate with turrets, gables, bays, fishscale shingles and many windows. One room in the house has four square walls. All others have angle walls or bay windows.

Adjacent to the house and in the middle of Ash Street is "Kate's tree," so called because of her defense of it nearly a hundred years ago. Mrs. Bailey obviously felt a commitment to preserve the tree from the mighty ax of city workers who had been given orders to cut the tree out of the city right-of-way. Mrs. Bailey proceeded to sit on her porch, with shotgun in hand, and dared any city worker to cut it down. That tree remains today, in the middle of Ash Street, due to the tenacity of Mrs. Bailey.

The Bailey family owned the home for almost 70 of its now 107 years. Since 1963, ownership has passed through five different families, all contributing their substantial monies and love to the home's continued preservation.

In 1973, the home was added to the National Register of Historic Places as an individual example of historic importance.

The Tom Hay family converted the house from a private residence to a bed and breakfast about 1982. Stained-glass windows were re-leaded, central heating and air installed, the roof replaced, and five new bathrooms constructed. The original home had but one. The original yellow pine floors, fireplaces, stained-glass windows, and pocket doors have been meticulously maintained.

Today, under new owners, it continues that 20-year tradition. Current guardians purchased the Bailey House in 1993. They converted the attic into three bedrooms and a comfortable den, where the innkeepers now reside.

Collection of S. Courtney McCranie

The tower and south elevation from the original architectural renderings.

The reception hall staircase lends grace to the Victorian aire.

The dining room at right, the front sitting parlor below, and the hearth hall opened to each other by large and heavy pocket doors, usually kept opened when the Bailey's entertained or simply to enhance air circulation during warm summer months. The pump organ in the dining area was used for family weddings and has been maintained over the years in perfect operating condition.

The parlor afforded a pleasant view across the veranda to Ash Street and passing friends and neighbors. Guests were received and entertained here and Kate Bailey would sing and play the piano for all to enjoy, even beyond the windows.

One of many suites of the Bailey family, adapted now for the comfort of bed-and-breakfast guests. This is the Amelia Room, located just off of the dining room and overlooking "Kate's tree."

One of the marks of a Queen Anne home is the elaborately styled chimney.

One of the many hearths of the Bailey house.

Hearth hall is lighted by the corner windows of the turret and these stained-glass masterpieces shining from across the staircase landing.

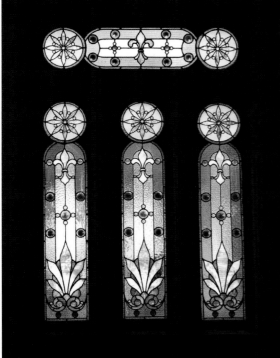

The ornate south tower.

Kate Bailey threatened city employees, nearly a hundred years ago, with the serious end of a shotgun when they approached to cut down an old oak tree peacefully growing older in the middle of Ash Street. No doubt Kate still watches over her now massive oak just a few dozen feet from her veranda rocker.

FAIRBANKS HOUSE

Circa 1890's

The magnificent Fairbanks house was designed in
the Italianate style and finished in 1885 for George
Rainsford Fairbanks, citrus industry pioneer,
educator, newspaper editor, and historian

Fairbanks House Collection.

Circa 1890's.

Many years have passed since Major George Fairbanks relaxed in the entrance hall of the home the family dubbed Fairbank's Folly. The entrance hall columns, arch, and elegant staircase areas were masterfully constructed of the finest of Honduran mahogany. Thought to be rather extravagant, the home had telephones, running water, concrete sidewalks, and the town's first elevator.

One of the grand old dames of Amelia Island is the Fairbanks House, originally the home of Major George R. Fairbanks, the politician and editor of Fernandina's *Florida Mirror* from 1879 to 1885. Fairbanks was known and respected as an honorable gentleman throughout Florida.

Fairbanks was born in Watertown, New York, and came to Florida where he served as State Senator from 1846 to 1848. During the War Between the States, he attained the rank of major and became Quartermaster of the Army of Tennessee. Following the war, he assisted in the founding of the University of the South at Suwanee, Tennessee, and organized and assumed the first presidency of the Florida Historical Society. He became a master of history, publishing *The*

Spaniards in Florida in 1868, the *History of Florida* in 1871, the *History of St. Augustine* in 1881, and the *History of the University of the South* in 1905. His achievements are many in law, business, and the public sector.

Fairbanks came to Fernandina in 1880 at the behest of David Yulee. He accepted the editorship of the *Florida Mirror*. He held that post for more than 10 years becoming one of the most respected newspaperman in the south.

In the mid-1880's, Fairbanks employed local architect, Robert Schuyler, to design the finest of homes in high-styled Italianate architectural style, three living-quarter stories encompassing 20 rooms and topped with a 10 by 10-foot tower.

Previous Page - The insert photograph was taken near the turn into the 20th century. Original colors were mustard yellow with deep green window trim and brick red window sash and arches, very close to its appearance today. (Photo courtesy Fairbanks House Collection)

The spacious front parlor with its ornate hearth and pine flooring which was originally covered with matting imported from China. Many rooms are joined with sliding pocket doors as those here connecting the parlor and the dining area.

The home's significant architectural features include its hallmark four-story tower, arcaded galleries, piazzas on three sides, arched and pediment windows, and bracketed cornices, all significant characteristics of the Italianate style. The original color scheme was mustard yellow with windows trimmed in deep green and arches trimmed in red - true to Victorian eccentricity.

On the main floor, Fairbanks had an entrance hall, parlor, dining room, library, and a guest bedroom. The floors were covered with matting imported from China. On the second floor were four bedrooms and a playroom over the kitchen. The third floor was an attic for storage and play for the kids. Noted by a Fairbanks descendent, "Every bedroom had a dressing room with a washstand, basin, pitcher, and a chamber pot. Rachel, the maid, emptied the slop bowls and chamber pots by way of the back stairs and cleaned them with ammonia."

The Fairbanks house sold to the Haile family during WWI at a bargain price and remained in that family until 1981. During the Haile tenure as guardians, the home was individually listed on the National Register of Historic Places in 1973. Having slipped into poor condition and in need of help, the home caught the eye of a team of Gainesville restoration enthusiasts in 1981, who purchased and began their year-and-a-half project. The 7,000 square-foot mansion was then divided into seven apartment units. All wiring, plumbing, and

Ten fireplaces adorn and warm the halls, parlors, and sleeping rooms of the estate. Two are framed with tiles depicting scenes from Shakespear's plays and Aesop's fables. Six others are carved of soapstone with intricate hand carvings. Fairbanks employed a full-time wood cutter to keep 10 fireplaces supplied with fuel. Wood was delivered a few blocks away by train then carted to the house before being lifted by one of the community's first elevators to wood boxes at each of the fireplaces.

The original kitchen was separate from the house and joined by a hallway. It has been converted to a living and sleeping suite as a part of the conversion to a bed and breakfast.

appliances were replaced or upgraded, roofing materials were replaced, and central heat and air conditioning added.

Today the edifice is lovingly maintained as one of the island's numerous bed and breakfasts. It is sometimes referred to as Fairbanks Folly and, along with the Hirth House on North 6th Street, is among the few pure examples of residential Italianate architecture in Florida.

At the rear of the Fairbanks property are two older cottages converted to guest rooms, the old carriage house and the old servant's quarters known as Hattie's House in years gone by. It reveals its genuine antiquity through its wood peg construction.

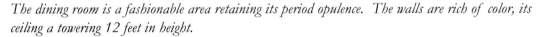

The dining room is a fashionable area retaining its period opulence. The walls are rich of color, its ceiling a towering 12 feet in height.

The true size of the house is realized when viewed from the south patio and pool area. The old and the new mix well.

Corner boxes or rosettes are above each door and window of the bedroom and are seen throughout the house.

Bedroom of a Fairbanks daughter on the second floor.

FLORIDA HOUSE

Although it never served as a private residence, the Florida House is one of the grand old antebellum buildings of Amelia Island and has always served as an inn.

The main structure was built by the Florida Railroad and opened its doors to the public somewhere between 1857 and 1859. It served its Florida Railroad owners with housing for employees, as well as the other guests traveling the rails. As with many of the buildings of the early days, skilled railroad carpenters and laborers were used in its construction.

Its architectural style is in the vernacular tradition with Greek Revival adaptations common to inns of the antebellum South. The design was a simple rectangular shape with a gabled roof parallel to street. The facade had double-galleried porches. Initially there were thirteen small rooms, an office, and little else.

Then came the Civil War, and by 1862, Union occupation of Amelia Island. With railroad employees scattered west to the security of the interior, the Union Army confiscated the building for housing.

Following the war, the hotel was acquired by Major Leddy, Union Provost Marshal at Fort Clinch, who operated the Florida House with his wife. Additions are believed to have been made during or just after the war. As reconstruction of the South proceeded, tourists began returning and Fernandina began a steady and sure growth. Following the Major's death, Mrs. Leddy continued on as the innkeeper. In 1882, with the island

The eight flags of Amelia Island fly over the full facade of today's Florida House Inn. The original 1850's hotel is in the center, with a large 1882 addition to the left. Below is the sitting room of the 1850's section of the house.

Transom and side lights of the 1850's hotel.

A patriotic theme accents this room in the pre-1882 addition to the house.

in the midst of its golden era, Mrs. Leddy had an adjoining building constructed, giving the inn a total of 25 rooms.

The inn remained in the Leddy family until 1940. The buildings had been deteriorating for years and continued so for many more. As with many of the nation's old homes and inns in 1920's and 1930's, the old Florida House was refitted as apartments, affording inexpensive housing to local residents at a difficult time.

Still operating as an apartment building in 1990, the old Florida House was sold and thus began a long process of restoration. Additions and upgrades brought new life to what was becoming the tired lady of Fernandina's venerable buildings. At present it continues to cater to Amelia Island's tourist trade in its original and gracious style.

A large patio is surrounded by the original Florida House and the pre-1882 addition to the right. The photograph is taken from a wing added in a recent restoration.

HOYT HOUSE

The Hoyt name was prominent in the business community of Fernandina's post Civil War years. Fred W. Hoyt came to Fernandina in 1879. He became a partner with W. A. Sanborn during the growth of the new fledgling Fernandina community. The Hoyt-Sanborn businesses were operated at 10 North 2nd Street and from one of Fernandina's showcase commercial buildings at Centre and 2nd Streets.

Unique to the Hoyt house is the double- door portico that is more common to homes in colder climates for wind and cold protection. This reflects Hoyt's New Hampshire background.

As a merchant, Hoyt sold hardware and building materials, groceries, and ship's stores at the North 2nd and Centre Street chandlery. Hoyt invested in real estate and founded the First National Bank of Fernandina and other financial institutions in Nassau and Duval Counties.

Fred Hoyt and his wife Kate had their home constructed by local contractor John R. Mann, who is said to have been modeled it after the Rockefeller Cottage on Jekyll Island. The Hoyt home is of balloon frame construction with a foundation of brick piers and was completed in 1905. The home is a frame vernacular structure with a colonial revival porch across the full length of the front and east side. Its design is significant for its octagonal two-story bay, hip roof and dormers, balcony, and bracketed eaves.

Fred Hoyt, his wife Kate, and their three children lived in the house for many years. Following Hoyt's death in 1925, the home was purchased by the Everett Mizell family who lived there for 50 years. It then was refitted in the 1970's as law offices. In 1993, the wonderful old dwelling was purchased and restored as one of the island's historic bed and breakfasts.

The front living area is a favorite gathering area for music and conversation. It commands a wide view of the elite corner property with its majestic oak. Note the picture moldings rather then fancy cornice.

The front sitting parlor viewing back through the elegant dining room.

The sitting parlor's front windows face Atlantic Avenue and the beautiful St. Peters Episcopal Church.

The newel post and the lighted figurine, tradition says, signifies that the mortgage has been satisfied.

MARCELLUS WILLIAMS HOUSE

Circa 1928

From the collection of Jack Hines, Jr.

This is a pearl of Amelia Island and Fernandina Beach architecture, a magnificent relic of antebellum times and the golden era of Amelia Island. New Fernandina was but a few years old when a native Bostonian had his home built circa 1856, on the outskirts of town.

With few exceptions, such as Centre and North 2nd Streets, there were no roads to speak of, only foot paths. The paths ran between the few homes and a scattering of general merchandise shops near the foot of Centre Street. Roads existed only on surveyors' plats drawn up for future development.

Disgruntled with talk of secession, the native Bostonian sold his new home to Marcellus Williams, who had come to East Florida in 1846 to survey and validate Spanish land grants. Marcellus remodeled what was of Greek Revival design to its present state. He planted large oaks along Ash and South 9th Streets.

Half a dozen years after the Civil War, Marcellus and his son, Arthur T. Williams, set out on a number of surveying ventures to south Florida where Marcellus surveyed throughout the area of Biscayne Bay. In 1870, Arthur recalled there were only 18 to 20 people living on the bay, and a scattering of Indians. Arthur made five trips to south

The veranda displays a throng of spindles and camphored posts that appear to go in all directions. Actually, all have a purpose in the support of the porch above.

Florida from Fernandina with his father in the early 1870's. He always returned with a lifetime of tales of the wild. In the years to come, Arthur built his home just one block away from his parents on the corner of South 10th and Ash Streets. That home remains today.

Little is substantiated of the lore that is associated with the Williams house. It is said that this was a safehouse on the underground railroad which gave passage to slaves on their way north. Supposedly the house has a hidden room where slaves were protected. Jefferson Davis is said to have stored some of his personal effects here and to have visited the house on several occasions. This now seems quite contrary to the fact that Marcellus was a Northerner who would hold no affection for Jefferson Davis.

Architecturally, the Williams house is a two-and-a-half-story frame vernacular residential structure significant for its two-story veranda heavily decorated with turned ornamentation, five stained-glass windows along the main staircase, and its floor-to-ceiling windows. This outstanding restored lady of the antebellum period is a modest 3700 square feet of charm.

The entry hall photographed from three directions captures the essence of a magnificent Victorian home.

Most common area rooms of the era were wide and spacious for entertaining friends and family. Rooms were usually separated only by double pocket doors that, when opened, increased air flow and accommodated large groups.

The front parlor mantle. Decorative hearths were a signature piece of the original owner, its design usually carefully thought out prior to its making.

For many years, the Williams family had a grand piano in the front parlor. The wonderful old instrument is now on display at the Amelia Island Museum of History.

Black walnut is found next to
yellow pine in molding and panels
of the more affluent of Victorian
era builders.

Brass light and door
fixtures are found in
many homes and
buildings of the era.

The early morning sun.

OLD FERNANDINA
Old Town

On the banks of the Amelia River is a settlement that is longing to replant the seeds of a community and start anew as the senior member of the Amelia Island family. Long ago, the area now known as Old Town gave up her right to be called Fernandina. Nearly 160 years have passed since the city fathers gave up on the historic site atop a bluff that had provided sanctuary to Native Americans, British and Spanish colonists, rebels of the sea, slave-traders, and early harbor pilots and fishermen.

The structures of this original Fernandina, once including several Spanish forts, no longer exist, save possibly two dwellings, the Pedro Ponce frame vernacular house at 819 Someruelos Street and the Domingo Estanochaly frame vernacular house at 16 Estrada Street. The rest have burned, rotted, or blown away from neglect. The only other elements that remain of the original town are its platted streets and notes of history now and then put in print.

One wonders why the dwellings of this Spanish town did not survive, as have the buildings of its sister community of the Spanish period, St. Augustine. The answer is twofold - available building materials and the nationality and traditions of those living in the community. The Spanish were inclined to build using masonry material such as tabby or coquina, materials that were readily available in the St. Augustine area. The newcomers searched the Amelia Island area for sufficient coquina but were unsuccessful. The resource that was available, however, was timber. A visitor to Fernandina noted in an 1817 Savannah newspaper that there were approximately forty houses, some two story, all made of wood.

Perhaps of greater influence on local building in the Spanish time period (1795 to 1817) was that most of the inhabitants of Spanish Fernandina were of English descent. Many were British loyalists who had moved south after the American Revolution. Many more were patriots of the new American government, who were taking advantage of relaxed citizenship requirements for the acquisition of land set forth by the Spanish government in the early 1790's. Both groups continued the English building tradition of wood-frame construction. Tabby, however, was occasionally used as a material for foundation piers.

From about 1821 until about 1853, Old Town Fernandina's growth was stagnated with little to no construction. The seat of county government was moved to the mainland in the 1830's and commercial ventures closed their doors and moved on. Many of the forty homes mentioned in the 1817 article went into disrepair and the town dwindled to a scattering of homes.

In 1853, Fernandina began to look forward to a dramatic resurgence in its economy when David Yulee announced that Fernandina would be the eastern terminus of a planned cross-state Florida Railroad. However, in the development stages, it was realized that the rails could not cross the swamp to the south of the community. Yulee's agents purchased land from the descendents of the Domingo Fernandez estate and located the terminal at what became the foot of Centre Street, giving birth to a new Fernandina. Streets were platted, and commercial development followed to the new location, extending north on 2nd Street.

Some residents remained on the hill of old Fernandina, many living in small cracker-style cottages along the water's edge. Others, seamen and harbor or bar pilots, built larger two-story homes with cupolas or towers that enabled them to see incoming vessels. One of them was built by Captain James Bell, topped with a small cupola from which he could climb out and watch incoming ship traffic. The old Captain's House, as it is called, now keeps watch over an open, grassy space known as the Plaza, the original location of Spanish Fort San Carlos. The Plaza stretches from Estrada Street to the edge of the bluff overlooking the Sound and provides the Captain's House with a magnificent view in all directions. Other harbor pilots, legend to Old Town, were Captain William Jones Davis, Captain William Sharpe, Captain McNeil, Captain Robert Downes, and Captain Tom Lasserre.

A fire house was built at 712 San Fernando Street, and a post office operated at various locations, at one time behind the Captain Downes house just west of the Plaza. On the southeast corner of San Fernando and Estrada Streets, harbor pilots maintained a lookout tower where they could see miles out to the open sea. Several churches served Old Town over the years. The Catholic church was on the southeast corner of the Plaza and the Episcopal church, known as the Seaman's Church, down on White Street. In the late 1920's, there were but two phones in Old Town, one at the McNeil house and one at the Downes house.

There are signs of a rebirth in recent years, re-nourishing some level of respect once given this orphaned community on the hill. Investors, undaunted by generations of the Old Town image, have borrowed, mortgaged, and labored at restoring a number of the old structures, most of them built since the Civil War. The new owners have fallen in love with Old Town's charm and historic significance.

Some of these restoration projects are visualized here in various stages of their renewed lives.

CAPTAIN'S HOUSE
ALSO KNOWN AS THE BELL OR DOWNES HOUSE

Since the early days of Spanish occupation the Plaza has always been the focal point of Old Fernandina. Across the street from the Plaza, on the southeast corner of White and Estrada Streets, is the story book, Victorian-age structure known as the Captain's House.

The view from the Captain's House is west across the open Plaza, and the site of old Fort San Carlos, destroyed many years ago. Looking from the embankment, it is difficult to envision the considerable activity that took place here 200 years ago with hundreds of tall ships, men-of-war, schooners, and vessels belonging to buccaneers of the high seas docked or anchored just off shore.

Harbor pilot and builder James Bell purchased the lot on the corner in the 1880's and completed his two-story house and tower in less than a year. Atop of the second floor he constructed his cupola to watch for incoming ships.

By 1903, the house sold to bar pilot Captain Robert H. Downes and has since passed through many family names. The Captain's House is noted in more recent times for its roll as the winsome home in the film production of *The New Adventures of Pippi Longstockings*.

The house is most noteworthy for its tower with shingled gable dormers, two-story bay windows, ornate hoods, cornices, verge boards, and brackets.

The side parlor is charming in its extension to the bay window centered with a baby grand, providing a view toward the new Fernandina. The central entrance hall (right) leads to the rear kitchen and the staircase leads to bedrooms above, that afford a panoramic view of the Amelia River and Cumberland Sound.

SWEARINGEN HOUSE

This home was built before the War Between the States but its history until the turn of the 20th century has been elusive. Most likely built by a harbor pilot, his name remains unknown. The Swearingen family lived here for many years, then the Vernon Jones family and by 1949, the Harold Fulford family had purchased the house and remained here until 2001.

The original design included a porch on the Ladies Street facade, but in restoration begun in 2001, these were removed and replaced with two-story, full verandas reaching around the entire length of the house on Amelia Street. Its shotgun design includes a hall to the rear, two rooms below (one now a kitchen), a staircase off of the hallway, two rooms on the second level, and a dormer bedroom on the third level.

The front sitting parlor.

The relocated kitchen retains its early roots in its pine ceiling, modest cornice, door casings and moldings.

The kitchen of old was beyond today's skylighted and open-beamed drafting room that now connects it to the house.

The original doweled balusters and hand rails of the second floor contrasts with the new spiraling staircase that leads to the third floor bedroom suite.

The little cottage near the intersection of White and Amelia Streets is a striking upgrade from its former image. A veranda now wraps the house and within is a refreshing reincarnation.

Before renovation.

HENDERSON COTTAGE

The fireplace below faced a small room to the front and, almost out of view to the right was, and still is, the kitchen.

The Henderson house was constructed in Old Town in 1911 and is pictured above just prior to its two-year revitalization which was begun in 1998. The house's transformation is amazing.

Its simple "shotgun-style" architecture was common to the period in all corners of the South. It had a small living and dining room, kitchen, and a hallway that led from the front to the rear door. In the rear of this home were two small bedrooms and a bath. These are believed to have been added years after the 1911 construction.

In the late 1990's redesign, the owner was intent on maintaining the integrity of the foundation but made massive changes to the internal room layout. The two fireplaces were kept intact, but disabled because of their condition. All interior walls were removed with the exception of those around the bathroom. The new open area became the spacious dining and living rooms and the kitchen.

An expansion of the second floor was made for sleeping, lounging, and office quarters. A 4-foot knee wall was added above the existing old 8-foot exterior walls and was crowned with a 14-foot gabled tin roof.

Two French doors replaced the original small entrance door and a veranda was added around the house and expanded the living space to the out-of-doors.

The late 1990's renovations such as the reincarnation of the Henderson house, were incentives to others who are proceeding with restoration projects of other historic homes of Old Town Fernandina.

A staircase was added to the new, expanded spaces above.

DANIEL KELLY COTTAGE

Restoration began in September of 2001 and continues more than a year later.

Legend has it that this old house began its long life in Old Town many years before being moved to new Fernandina where it remained for many years.

Researched by the *Fernandina News-Leader* in the late 1980's, the paper noted "it is generally believed that the house was built in 1856 by Daniel Kelly who came to Fernandina from Ireland." It was later inherited by his niece, Elize Kelly Brady, who lived in it for some time before making it a rental.

In the 1930's, it became a boarding house with a kitchen that fed more than its boarders. Times were tough in the 1930's, and as a result hot meals at 25 to 50 cents were in big demand. The two paper mills were under construction and so the town was overflowing with construction workers who slept in tents and shanties with no cooking facilities.

Three stages of restoration can be seen in these photographs above taken approximately 3 months apart. The owner/restorer uses architectural salvage to complete the second floor porch below and the mantle at left.

The News-Leader was purchased by the New York Times in 1973 and, in turn, the paper purchased their present building and the next door property where the cottage sat. In the years that followed, the cottage was leased to a variety of businesses.

In December of 1988, the cottage was moved back to Old Town across from the Plaza, where it would be restored. Years passed, but the task finally came to fruition after it was moved to the corner of Amelia and White Streets. Restoration began at the beginning of this new century in 2001.

Photographs here show the progress and rebirth of what is fondly called the "little cottage from the News-Leader parking lot."

CAPTAIN SHARPE HOUSE

Captain William Sharpe was one of the harbor pilots who were so much a part of Old Town's population. The construction date and builder are unknown but one of its first inhabitants was Captain Sharpe.

Its architectural attributes are in its rectangular design with a two-storied gallery porch and its gabled roof, common to Southern homes before and after the Civil War.

An addition was added to the rear more then a hundred years ago, housing the kitchen and several other rooms. A fire nearly destroyed the house many years ago, from fireplace cinders that caught the wood shingle roofing, burning out the third floor bedroom.

Restoration on the house began in 2001 and is ongoing. The two storied porch on the left above is a recent addition, lathe and plaster walls have been replaced, and the roof is now metal. The house continues its full restoration with a kitchen addition planned for the future.

The hearth in the midst of restoration.

The entry hall and the front parlor.

CAPTAIN MCNEIL HOUSE

Here is found a marvelous Folk Victorian which was, at one time, the home of harbor pilot McNeil. Restoration began about 1990, and continues twelve years later. The two-and-a-half-story wood-frame home has a high pitch Gothic Revival style roof with gabled dormers, a Italianate style, square bay window, and modestly fanciful pine molding and trim throughout.

The original unattached kitchen wing at the rear remains as the owner's restoration workshop. The wood stove, kitchen water supply and cooking utensils were relocated to the inside of the house many years ago.

FERNANDINA'S COMMERCIAL DISTRICT

Fernandina has experienced a unique 200-year-old growth pattern. Its geographic location and subsequent development traveled down the hill from the little community now referred to as Old Town, to the present town's North 2nd Street with the arrival of the railroad. Then, the great fire of 1876 pushed it over to Centre Street, where government offices and buildings, retail shops, and the learning centers followed as history progressed. What remains of that evolution today is a community focused on an east/west Centre Street commercial district, with residential areas spread north and south.

This section of Tidewater Amelia focuses on many of the old buildings that survive from that evolution and how they have been adapted to today's life-style. What is seen on this and the following pages are brick and mortar commercial buildings constructed after the fire of 1876. The only exception featured in this book is the Kydd building at Centre and 3rd Streets, a survivor of that great conflagration.

Commercially, the majority of the historically significant structures have been radically altered on the interiors to meet the demands of individual owners over the years. Exteriors, however, are governed by historic district codes and are protected from out-of-era changes.

The wood-frame commercial buildings of Old Town and most of North 2nd Street are gone. Also, the early wood structures of Centre Street are no more. Fire, weather, neglect, and a lack of historical appreciation in the first 70 years of the 20th century took a tremendous toll on Fernandina's (and America's) inventory of aging architecture.

Significant to the exterior design among these buildings is a predominance of the Italianate style and the use of cast iron on the facades which increased the structural stability and were simply fashionable. Cast iron was a mass-produced, American architectural innovation of the 19th century. It was cheaper than ornamental stone or brick. It garnished structures and allowed ornate features to be prefabricated from molds in foundries. Cast iron permitted designers to build larger windows on all floors, thus bringing natural light where there was none. This is a sampling of what survives in all areas of exterior design.

Sanborne & Hoyt Building

W. A. Sanborn and Fred W. Hoyt established a grocery, ship chandlery, grain, furniture, and building materials business in 1870. The business was later passed on to Fred's son Charles L. Hoyt in partnership with W. O. Jeffreys and was moved to a new location at 10 North 2nd Street in 1882 to a building constructed by William John Lohman. The building has a facade of fanciful cast iron.

The firm was known as Fred W. Hoyt & Company and grew into the city's second largest business. The firm expanded its sales and dealings to include northeast Florida, doing a large amount of business along the Florida Transit Railroad and along the St. Marys River.

Starke Building

Duryee Building

3rd and Centre Streets.

The Angel building at Centre and North 3rd Streets housed the bakery and grocery of Charles Angel when first constructed in the days following the fire of 1876.

The Swann Building at 4th and Centre Streets.

Palace Saloon billboard.

The parapet, brackets and ornate cornice of the Swann building.

300 Block of Centre Street.

205 Centre Street.

Oriel windows originated in the early Gothic or Tudor periods, and in this case, they lie beneath a castellated parapet.

The 300 block of Centre Street.

The 200 block of Centre Street.

A pilastered brick column in the 100 block of Centre Street.

COMMERCIAL

A fading sign of the past in the 100 block of Centre Street.

The Lohman building on Ash Street.

A parapet in the 300 block of Centre Street.

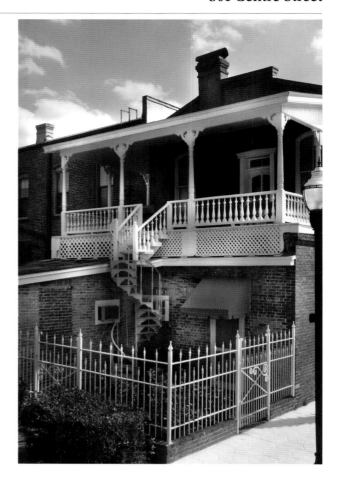

THE KYDD BUILDING

The 1870's brought a construction boom to Fernandina. In 1873, James and Thomas Kydd constructed the first brick building in new Fernandina. The bricks proved their worth when the fire of 1876 spared the Kydd investment. Only Fort Clinch and the Amelia lighthouse preceded the Kydd building with the use of masonry.

Its design has many features of Italianate influence such as a bracketed parapet, decorative brick moldings and sills, arched window openings, and a cast-iron facade. The use of iron in building construction began just after the Civil War and lasted until about 1910. Some of the best surviving examples are found in the commercial buildings of Centre Street, especially with the Swann, Hoyt, and Kydd buildings.

The first floor interior walls and ceiling of the Kydd building are covered with pressed tin, popular in the late 19th century as a relatively inexpensive covering. Most commercial buildings along Centre Street have renovated or modernized interiors and relatively few have kept the charm of the original materials that at one time covered the majority of ceilings.

Thomas Kydd and his wife lived on the second floor where they enjoyed the advantages of being near the business and having an in-town home.

The large arched back-bar is supported by two undraped caryatids or figurine columns as shown at the left. The entire back bar was carved by German craftsmen from black mahogany and English oak and purchased by Hirth nearly one hundred years ago for $1400.

With the death of Louis Hirth in 1938, the palace operated as a part of the Hirth estate until 1957. Purchased by two local businessmen, the Palace experienced a major restoration including repair of the murals by the artist who had originally painted them.

The second restoration of the Palace has been accomplished since the fire of 1999, a near deathblow that many thought could not be overcome.

THE PALACE SALOON

A Yankee lieutenant by the name of Josiah Prescott, who had been part of the Union occupying forces of the War Between the States, returned to Amelia Island following the war. By 1878, he constructed a brick building at the corner of 2nd and Centre Streets and opened a boot and shoe store. The design embodied the Italianate architectural influence with its arched windows and door openings and its decorative cornices and window hoods.

A young German immigrant by the name of Louis G. Hirth arrived in the mid-1890's, and in the ensuing years he forever changed the image of the Prescott building. At first, Hirth was a bartender for J. J. Rutishauser, but soon opened his own bar, The Trilby, on North 3rd Street.

Desiring to cater to the elite, Hirth purchased the Prescott building for $5500 with $1500 down. He proceeded to lavishly refit with embossed tin ceilings, marble, mahogany, oak, brass, and fine art. He enlisted the help of the now famous brewer Adolphus Busch in securing English oak fixtures in what was called the St. Louis exposition style, elaborate bar furniture that survives today. The end result was the Palace Saloon.

In its early years, the Palace hosted the Carnegies of Cumberland Island, the Rockefellers, du Ponts, Pulitzers, and the Morgans. Even Henry Ford and Samuel Goldwyn are said to have pushed through the swinging bar doors. However, the clientele were primarily the ship captains and local well-to-do, playing cards in the rooms above or sipping suds or a shot of whiskey at the bar. It was known to all as a "gentleman's establishment."

The Palace Saloon, is now as deeply anchored in the history of Fernandina, as a ship is to the harbor. It survives today as the oldest liquor establishment in Florida under the same name, at the same location.

The brass cash register was used only with visitors, as tabs were kept for local patrons who were billed at the end of the month. A large draft was 5 cents and a bottle of Scotch a dollar fifty.

Paintings have adorned the walls of the Palace since its opening. Hirth commissioned Roy Kennard of Jacksonville who painted six murals which, unfortunately, were heavily damaged in the devastating fire that swept the building in 1999. With the restoration of the Palace over the next two years, the Kennard paintings were skillfully revived along the walls of the Palace. Kennard's mural of Shakespear's "Falstaff" can be seen at the far end of the bar. Another of Kennard's murals was "Proving It By The Book." The images of the pirates, near the pub's entrance is entitled "Stand and Deliver."

Proving It By The Book.

Stand And Deliver.

After the fire in 1999, the old package store adjacent to the Palace on Centre Street was consolidated within the Palace as a dance and entertainment hall and it was restored to somewhat mirror the image of the Palace. A period bar that had been stored on the second floor of the Palace was brought down and custom fitted along the west wall. An old jukebox was rejuvenated and a bandstand was put into place.

CHANDLERY / HOYT BUILDING

The Chandlery is at the crossroads of commercial development at Centre and North 2nd Streets. It takes its name from the ship's chandlery that occupied the building for many years after its 1879 construction.

In the 1850's and 1860's commercial buildings at this site and all along Centre and 2nd Streets were fabricated of wood, falling prey to the great fire of 1876. Immediately following the fire, having learned a horrible lesson of the effect of a disaster such as this on economics, the town began reconstruction with brick and mortar.

The building was built by and originally housed the A. B. Noyes grocery. It was but two stories high. The firm of Horsey & Co., druggists and chemists, occupied a 20 foot by 60 foot apartment, presumably one section of first floor, in the 1870's and 1880's. Noyes sold the building to Fred Hoyt who brought in a chandlery, hence the name Chandlery was adapted to the building years later. Hoyt later sold to D. A. Kelly and his brothers who operated a wholesale and retail grocery house known as D. A. Kelly Co.

The Chandlery is the tallest commercial building in new Fernandina, restored now to its 19th-century charm. Heart pine trim is everywhere, having matured for hundreds of years in the forests of mainland Florida. It will beautify the halls of the Chandlery for many years to come.

At the turn of the 20th century, fire damaged the building extensively, compelling its owners to rebuild. The interior was restored and, with a local economy still in high gear, a third story was added. The first level retail facade was then modernized with large glass windows for display of goods.

The Chandlery exhibits Italianate features in its arched windows and door openings, and decorative brickwork on cornices, and window hoods. In recent restoration, the first floor facade was returned to its classic 19th-century appearance. The upper floors once warehousing chandlery goods now provide office space in a historic atmosphere.

From an entrance on North 2nd Street you enter the lobby and ascend an imposing grand staircase to the upper floors. Newel posts, balusters, handrails, and moldings on the staircase are all of heart pine, alluding to its late 19th-century construction. The interior of the outside walls have been stripped to the Georgia clay brick, removed of lathe and plaster, leaving it a rustic early Fernandina appearance.

BELL'S BEECH STREET HOUSE

In 1889, Captain William Bell constructed this house after completing several other houses in Old Town. Like his twin brother, James, William was a harbor pilot by trade whose talents were given to construction in times of slow harbor activity. This is one of many homes that William and his brother built on Amelia Island

An Eastlake frame residential design, the obvious architectural features of this Bell house are its two-story verandah with Chippendale balustrades and large two-story bay windows. Though both of the brothers participated in the construction of the house, it was built by William as a gift for his bride.

The home is constructed of heart pine, with a metal roof, and marble mantels and fireplace facades imported from Italy. William lived out his life here, passing away in 1915.

During the depression years, the home was converted to an apartment house with additions being made to the side and rear. It continued on as an apartment house until the Bell family sold in 1972, when it was converted for retail use.

In 1990, two partners from Boston purchased the Bell house. They also purchased the adjoining houses where they establish the Beech Street Grill. In 1992, the main house was converted from the 'C' House Gift and Shell Shop to today's version of the Beech and a new life began for the "Grande Dame of Beech Street."

The Bell house entrance hall now welcomes dining guests with soft light from bay windows, and pine newel post and spindled balusters leading to dining spaces above.

The upstairs sleeping rooms of Bell family are now consolidated into one large dining room of the Beech Street Grill restaurant. Marble facades grace the old fireplaces and window moldings and cornices replicate the simpler embellishments of the time.

C.H. HUOT BUILDINGS

Today the Standard Marine Supply Corporation is housed in the C.H. Huot Building at 101 North 2nd Street.

The Frenchman C. H. Huot came to America in 1852 and to Fernandina in 1857 and was soon identified with many business interests. At an early date, C. H. and his partner, brother Dr. L. V. Huot, who remained for a time in Paris, established a business on Centre Street as Huot & Co. They later built a store at 101 North 2nd Street, the location of today's Standard Marine Supply, and operated a ship's chandlery. The business existed until the great fire of 1876 leveled the area.

Two years after the fire, they built a warehouse at 12 North 2nd Street, now the 1878 Restaurant. Four years later, the brothers rebuilt on their original site at 101 North 2nd.

This site was again used as a ship's chandlery but this time they constructed a massive 101 by 40 foot structure of Philadelphia brick, with two stories and a third floor cupola. The entire first floor was used as a store, the west and south sides for dry goods, while the north side was for general merchandise. On the east side was Mr. Huot's office and a semicircular counter for two clerks and a bookkeeper. Huot offered space at these counters for captains to pay their crews and stevedores. The second floor was split into six rooms and used for storage.

The character of a building can be seen in fanciful hood designs.

Over the years, the 101 2nd Street location served as a place for the Sisters of St. Joseph's convent to sell their handmade goods. Steamship agents used it as a warehouse, and during WWII it was a tent factory .

A leading business man, C. H. Huot also owned a nearby lumber mill that employed 25 people. The mill produced 25,000 feet of lumber a day.

In the 1950's, the Hardee brothers bought the building and established Standard Marine Supply which essentially returned the site to that of a chandlery.

The 12 North 2nd Street site is where Huot's assets increased dramatically. On the ground floor he operated a dry goods warehouse where local merchants could buy goods brought into the harbor on ship. Huot furnished part of the warehouse as a lounge for captains with all the latest maritime publications and a library that is said to have been the seed for the first library in Fernandina.

The second floor housed two apartments for the families of the Huot brothers. They lived there until 1882, when they had made their fortune, sold their businesses, and returned to their native France.

The next tenants of 12 North 2nd Street were the Kelly brothers who operated a feed and grocery until 1930. By the mid-1940's, it became a woodworking shop and later a furniture store. In 1974, the building was converted to a restaurant and has continued, except for short periods, to be used for that purpose.

The marine chandlery.

Time takes its toll on walls of lathe and plaster.

This was the heart of commercial Fernandina when constructed in 1878. The 1876 fire had taken its toll and the town was on a fast track back into the Victorian era.

The exterior of 12 N. 2nd Street Huot building eluded the stucco coating given its sister building in the early 1900's.

The restaurant that has replaced Huot's dry goods warehouse still carries an aire of antiquity though serving the public in an unrelated fashion. Open ceilings have been covered and plastered and lathe and plaster removed from the walls. A feeling of maritime appeal still hangs in the air.

In the days of old, many owners and operators lived in spaces above their establishments, as did C. H. Huot and his family at the 12 North 2nd Street location. The second floor hearths that heated the apartments remain as reminders of their private lives.

DOTTERER BUILDING

The intersection of Centre and 2nd Streets was laid waste by the fire of 1876. The entire area consisted of commercial structures built entirely of wood just before and after the War Between the States.

A. B. Noyes constructed a large two-story brick building on the northeast corner of Centre and 2nd Streets, to house his grocery business. On the northwest corner, in 1878, Josiah Prescott built a two-story building which housed a boot and shoe store (now the Palace Saloon). New brick buildings were going up in all directions up and down Centre Street and several blocks to the north on 2nd Street.

Along came Henry Eason Dotterer from Charleston, South Carolina. Dotterer was a Harvard graduate, a civil engineer,

and a veteran of the South Carolina Volunteers in the War Between The States. He was greatly impacted by his role as a foot soldier with General Lee's Army of Virginia at the Appomattox surrender of 1865. His health broken at the South's last stand, he walked back to his family at Charleston and endured many months of recuperation. He entered the mercantile business, packed his family and all of his worldly goods, and moved further south to the quiet beauty of Amelia Island to begin anew.

Little is known of their first 10 years on Amelia Island, but by 1876 and the great fire, he joined with others to rebuild the commercial district. Dotterer acquired the southwest corner of Centre and 2nd Streets and built his two-story vernacular in 1878. On the first floor he opened and operated the H. E. Dotterer Grocery, advertising fine family groceries and provisions.

The exterior of the Dotterer store displayed an array of corbeled brick ornamentation, tall 2-on-2, clear-glass, sashed windows, and large display windows facing on Centre Street. On the second floor was the office of Samuel Swann, one of the leading promoters of Fernandina in the latter part of the 19th century. A native of North Carolina, Swann had come to Fernandina in 1855 as an accountant for the firm building the new Florida Railroad. Swann lived in Cuba during the Civil War acting as a purchasing agent for the Confederacy's war effort. Returning to Fernandina following the war, Swann invested in lumber and real estate, was appointed Special Agent to the Governor of Florida, and was a Trustee of the Internal Improvement Fund of Florida.

Samuel Swann controlled his many interests from the corner offices overlooking the Chandlery and Prescott's Boot and Shoe Store, later the Palace Saloon.

The west wall of the Swann offices appears to have had the only fireplace on the second floor. The fireplace is now retired to the life of a decoration in space still used as an office.

THE SEYDEL BUILDING

The red brick used in the construction of the post-fire period was covered with stucco in the 1930's, believed to be an effort to modernize.

The Seydel Building was constructed the year following Fernandina's fire of 1876. The inscription above the second story windows reads "A. Seydel & Brothers, 1877." The German brothers had the building constructed along North 2nd Street, then known as the main street of Fernandina. On the first floor were two businesses, one a general store and the other a millinery and notions store. Both were owned by the Seydel brothers. Above were two apartments where the brothers and their families lived.

The second floor continued as private residences until the late 1930's, when it was converted to offices of the Bailey-Davis Steamship Agents. The first floor saw use as offices of the Nassau County Leader, a plumbing shop, an antique shop, and a labor union headquarters. Today, the entire building houses a favorite island restaurant, The Crab Trap.

The banister at the head of the staircase leading to the upstairs apartments is crafted of black walnut and remains as a part of the Crab Trap's second floor dining area decor. In the center of the building is another black walnut staircase leading to the attic and, at one time, was passage to an observation deck on the roof. The upstairs apartment floors are yellow pine and are original to the 1870's construction.

Two narrow balconies stretched across the back of the building where the families could sit and watch harbor activity or sunsets across the Amelia River. Iron brackets supported the balcony and though the balcony is now gone, most of the brackets remain. A wooden staircase went to the ground where the families maintained a courtyard and garden.

The two large family apartments were heated with fireplaces in each of the rooms. Several can be seen today by the patrons of the second floor dining room. The existing brick walls were originally covered with lathe and plaster, and the fireplaces had ornate wood mantles.

U.S. POST OFFICE, CUSTOMS & FEDERAL COURTHOUSE

The Federal Building today houses the United States Post Office but, in its early days, also housed the U.S. District Federal Court, U. S. Customs offices and military recruiting offices. The building was completed and dedicated in 1912. Architect for the federal project was James Knox Taylor and the building contractor was the D.J. Phipps Company of Newport News, Virginia. Cost of the project was $90,000.

What today is referred to as the post office building is significant for its unique Italian Renaissance revival architecture with heavy Mediterranean influences and the first use of steel frame construction on Amelia Island. Exterior design signatures are its overhanging eaves, the barrel tile roof, a low-pitched hipped roof with arched dormers, and its arcaded Centre Street entrance.

Postcard dated 1916.

Little has changed since the initial years after its construction. Though the original palm trees are still in place along the sidewalk, the flag now flies from a ground-level pole. The window awnings have long since been removed and railings have been added down the entrance staircases.

U.S. Library of Congress, Historic American Building Survey

Restoration has returned courtroom chandeliers to their original elegance.

Architectural courtroom elevation dated 1909 matched to the present restored door and pediment above.

The grand staircase leads to legal offices and the two-story courtroom, restored but no longer hosting federal court proceedings.

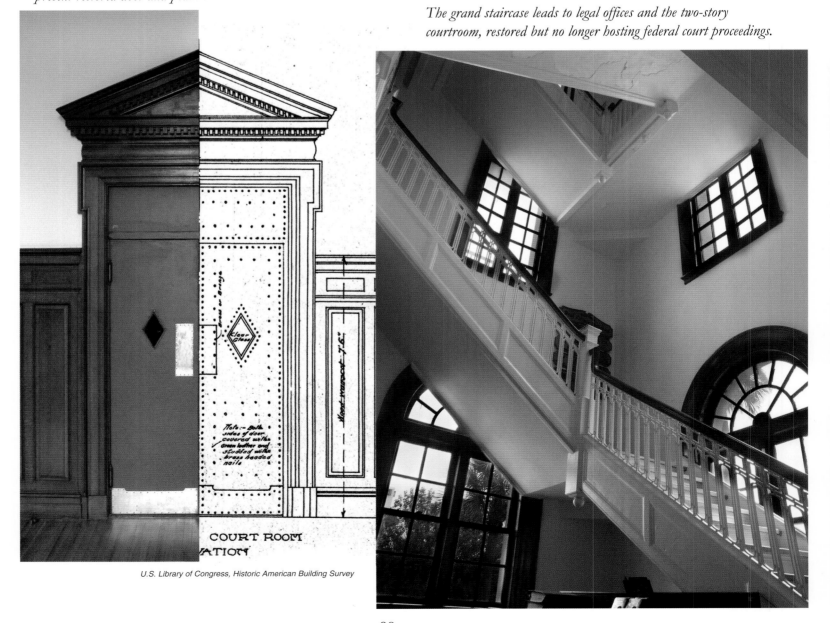

U.S. Library of Congress, Historic American Building Survey

98

NOTE —
Directory Board
on other side of Door
Similar.

Incised letters

BULLETIN

Clear Glass.

obscure Glass.

Wood

Marble Base

No. 130.

MASTER

MASTER

DIRECTORY

POSTMASTER
JIM FOSTER

SUPERVISORS OF CUSTOMER SERVICE
GARY POPLIN
VICTOR BLACKWELL

CONTRACT STATIONS

HAMILTON PRESS

COOPERS COFFEE SHOP
AMELIA ISLAND PLANTATION

First level entrance to the postmaster's office aligned to the 1909 architectural drawings.

Ornate detailed of the entablature above the west entrance.

Pilasters, or flat columns, frame the beautifully crafted and carved west portal. An iron balustrade caps the arched entrance.

NASSAU COUNTY COURTHOUSE

An indenture dated July 1, 1891 discloses the sale of land constituting lots 13, 14, and 15, each measuring 50 feet in width and 150 feet in depth. The amount of the transaction between the county and the seller, local merchant Henry E. Dotterer, was $2500. Jacksonville architect Alfred McClure's design fees came to $300, including three site visits. The commission negotiated with local contractor, William Mann, who agreed to $20,614 for construction.

Nassau County Court House - Fernandina Beach, Fla.

The Nassau County Courthouse is the dominant or pivotal structure of Fernandina's Centre Street. It towers above all other structures and can be seen furthest from any direction. Although, not the eldest of structural antiquity, it is now a model of historic restoration.

The history of the Nassau County Courthouse dates to the 1820's, shortly after Florida was acquired from Spain. The first building was situated on the Old Town bluff.

In 1835, due to the lack of activity in Fernandina, the courthouse was relocated to the settlement of Evergreen, north of Yulee on what today is County Road 108, to better serve other interior communities.

In 1862, the Civil War forced county officials to move it even further inland, to the Kings Highway, to keep the records out of the hands of occupying Union troops. Following the war, a Florida statute returned the courthouse to the new Fernandina.

In 1876, a great fire consumed Fernandina's waterfront and everything east to 3rd Street, destroying the heart of commercial Fernandina including the North 2nd Street courthouse offices. Those offices were located next door to what today is the Seydel Building (Crab Trap Restaurant).

In 1891, the Board of County Commissioners contracted the accomplished

Granite embellishments imported from New England were used in limited form for curbing, coping, sills, and other architectural features. Cast iron such as these of Corinthian columns where common to nineteenth century buildings yielding great compressive strength, lending themselves well in vertical structures such as the facade of the Nassau County Courthouse.

architectural firm of Ellis & McClure of Jacksonville to design a permanent and fitting county courthouse to be located at 416 Centre Street. Construction began in November of 1891 and was essentially completed by May of 1892. The primary construction contract was awarded to Fernandina contractor William Mann, assisted by his brother John R. Mann, who completed the project for $25,036, over budget by some $5,000.

The Nassau County Courthouse is a structure with influences of the Italianate architectural style in its windows, and Colonial Revival in its roof and facade. The structure is noteworthy for its Christopher Wren style cupola, bracketed cornice, brick pilasters, tall full-arched windows, hood moldings, granite sills, and arcaded entrances with cast-iron columns.

As best articulated in the historic district master site file, "Beyond its architectural significance, the Nassau County Courthouse embodies the political and commercial importance which the county seat represented to small Florida communities, such as Fernandina, during the late nineteenth and early twentieth centuries. It has always been essential to the economic vitality of Centre Street, particularly to the local merchants, lawyers, title and abstract companies, and others who do their business there. It has served Nassau County well since its construction, housing various public offices without interruption. It is a local landmark and considered to be one of the finest courthouse buildings in Florida."

Several years ago, because of decaying materials and safety concerns, the Courthouse cupola was removed and replicated with modern materials, esthetically returning the spire to the original design of the 1890's.

On March 7, 1997, the Auchter Company of Jacksonville began a massive remodeling project that took over five years to complete. In ceremonies held on Saturday, June 1, 2002, the Board of County Commissioners, the Clerk of Circuit and County Courts, and the 4th Judicial Circuit Court judges rededicated the courthouse to the citizens of Nassau County. It is the second oldest courthouse used for that purpose in the State of Florida.

The magnificently restored Nassau County Courthouse with its ornate speaker's balcony where political speeches have flowed forth and proclamations declared, and three-time Presidential candidate William Jennings Bryant once spoke.

Ribbon cutting ceremonies at the June 1, 2002 rededication honored Mrs. Celeste Kavanaugh, descendent of County Judge Hinton James Baker who played the major role in construction of the original 1890's courthouse. The Board of County Commissioners, County Constitutional Officers, and Judicial members officiated and assisted in the cutting of the ribbon.

The prisoners' staircase to the rear of the second floor courtroom remains but only for architectural integrity of the original design. With the 2002 restoration, the passage at the head of the staircase was sealed because of a rearrangement of prisoner holding rooms above. As with the fate of many of its users in the past, its purpose leads nowhere.

A simple brick window hood.

The original courthouse furnishings were supplied by Clark and Loftus Company for a modest $2,050, with courtroom chairs by J. W. Mason and Company at an undisclosed additional cost.

A view from the bench.

A little used staircase to the attic level is lighted through amber and rose glass.

The bell tower appears to reach to the clouds as it once again nurtures the legal community of Nassau County.

Though the interior furnishings were said to be simplistic, there were exceptions in delicately carved rail and newel posts, balusters, and door panels.

The bell, molded by Menceli & Company of West Troy, New York, was removed prior to the restoration and is now retired and on display on the first floor.

AMELIA LIGHT

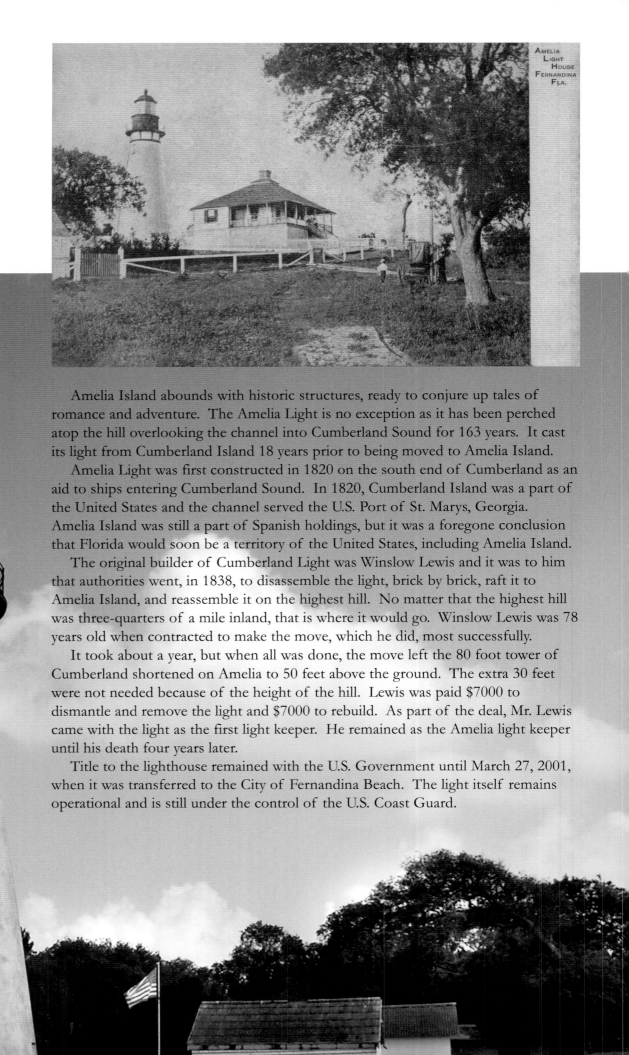

AMELIA
LIGHT
HOUSE
FERNANDINA
FLA.

Amelia Island abounds with historic structures, ready to conjure up tales of romance and adventure. The Amelia Light is no exception as it has been perched atop the hill overlooking the channel into Cumberland Sound for 163 years. It cast its light from Cumberland Island 18 years prior to being moved to Amelia Island.

Amelia Light was first constructed in 1820 on the south end of Cumberland as an aid to ships entering Cumberland Sound. In 1820, Cumberland Island was a part of the United States and the channel served the U.S. Port of St. Marys, Georgia. Amelia Island was still a part of Spanish holdings, but it was a foregone conclusion that Florida would soon be a territory of the United States, including Amelia Island.

The original builder of Cumberland Light was Winslow Lewis and it was to him that authorities went, in 1838, to disassemble the light, brick by brick, raft it to Amelia Island, and reassemble it on the highest hill. No matter that the highest hill was three-quarters of a mile inland, that is where it would go. Winslow Lewis was 78 years old when contracted to make the move, which he did, most successfully.

It took about a year, but when all was done, the move left the 80 foot tower of Cumberland shortened on Amelia to 50 feet above the ground. The extra 30 feet were not needed because of the height of the hill. Lewis was paid $7000 to dismantle and remove the light and $7000 to rebuild. As part of the deal, Mr. Lewis came with the light as the first light keeper. He remained as the Amelia light keeper until his death four years later.

Title to the lighthouse remained with the U.S. Government until March 27, 2001, when it was transferred to the City of Fernandina Beach. The light itself remains operational and is still under the control of the U.S. Coast Guard.

The original oil lamps were replaced in 1867 with what is called a third order Fresnel lens and replaced again in 1903. The lens remains in use today. The light and its rotating system were electrified in 1933.

The tower is dual-walled in that it has an outer wall that you see from outside, tapering toward the top. It measures 22 feet at the ground and 10 feet 6 inches at the top. The inside wall is a cylinder 9 feet in diameter from bottom to top. It supports the 69 granite steps as they spiral to the peak. The granite steps were imported from New England nearly 200 years ago. The wood casing to the left holds the cable and weight system that originally rotated the lens.

The oil house still sits at the base of the old lighthouse. Though cracked from ground settlement, it serves as a reminder of the early days when the Amelia Light was fueled by whale oil and kerosene. When electricity replaced the fuels in 1933, the little old oil house was reduced to a storage building.

FORT CLINCH

STATE PARK

Construction of a fort on the northern coast of Amelia Island began in 1847 as protection of one of the Southeast's more important deep water ports. It was named for General Duncan Lamont Clinch, a prominent figure in Florida's Seminole War of the 1830's, and built to military standards referred to as Totten's 3rd System of Fortifications. She would be a part of the Atlantic coastline system of defense of the United States.

The fort had not been completed by the outbreak of the Civil War in 1861, when the fort was taken over by forces of the Florida Militia. Following the invasion of the Union fleet in 1862, construction was resumed but again not completed by war's end.

Following the war, work went on but was permanently halted within a few years. The military operation of the garrison was greatly reduced and eventually ceased altogether. The fort was, however, reactivated in 1898 for several months during the Spanish-American War.

By 1926, the Federal government sold the fort, after which it passed through several private ownerships. By the 1930's, the fort was still intact but the doors, windows, roofs, and chimney tops were gone. The fort had been isolated, virtually abandoned, and overrun by nature.

In 1935, the State of Florida purchased the fort and 243 surrounding acres to develop one of its first state parks. The Civilian Conservation Corps (C.C.C.) did the initial work, digging out 10,000 cubic yards of sand, killing rattlesnakes, building roads, and removing cactus. The Corps took what was a jungle and developed it into a park that was opened to the public in 1938.

In 1957, Duncan Lamont Clinch's grandson donated $12,000 to the Duncan Lamont Clinch Historical Society to restore the prison and headquarters. By 1958, this was accomplished. In 1963, a $250,000.00 grant provided funds to repair the closures of the remaining buildings which was finished by 1966. The restoration is recorded by photographs in this book.

Today, Fort Clinch is a monument to America's past, a picture of our history, in a remarkable state of preservation.

The double smithy or blacksmith shop is partially covered with a barrel vault or single arch ceiling. This is a static display where the smithy and the farrier (horse blacksmith) once worked and today a reenactment has a farrier light the forge three times a week to demonstrate its use to visitors. The forge is believed to have been in the original inventory more than 150 years ago.

The second floor of the barracks which then held bunks three levels high. Rafters above supported a floor and a stand-up attic.

This view looks north across the roof of the bakery, blacksmith shops and the barracks. Cumberland Island is in the distance. Even in utilitarian structures such as these, designers incorporated a reasonable degree of artistic balance when aligning windows where walls or fireplaces are placed within the building's interior. The appearance of a fake window with granite sills and lentils such as those on the end of the barracks preserve the architectural symmetry of the wall. The first floor was bomb-proofed with brick arches. This is the only barracks ever completed at Fort Clinch.

Brick used in the construction of Fort Clinch came from a number of sources in two different time periods. Pre-Civil War brick, or that used before 1862, called Savannah Gray, is a regional brick of southeast Georgia. Its color is actually brown. The fort was only partially completed before the war. After Union troops occupied Amelia Island in 1862, U.S. Army Engineers were unable to acquire Southern brick. They shipped in what was required. The imported bricks were one-third smaller, harder, and have a red tone.

The floor in this southwest bastion is slate block 4 to 5 inches thick. Below is a cistern 12 feet in diameter with a 2,500 gallon capacity. Though it can't be seen without lifting the slate, the cistern is constructed of two layers of multiple or compound arches somewhat similar to the arching of the ceiling. The bastions are a mass with arches both above and below the floor. The fort has five bastions, each having a similar brick and vaulting system with cisterns.

Arching or vaulting was considered an essential ingredient to support heavy loads above, and protect from incoming cannon fire. The southwest bastion is the best display of arching. The photograph here shows multiple arches or what is called compound arching. There are four aches coming together forming a cross, then four more totaling an array of eight compound arches. Six are seen in this photograph. All are under the overhead gun-mount positions.

These windows to the outside walls are called embracers or ports. The lower square openings were for cannons and the tall vertical opening for riflemen. Several rifleman would use the vertical port, one a little higher and a little further back from the other. The view was straight down the exterior wall giving a clear shot at anyone trying to scale that wall.

The most ornate tunnel in the fort complex is this bomb proof barrel vault. Here are three distinct arches designed to protect the defenders from heavy bombardment.

NASSAU COUNTY JAIL
AMELIA ISLAND MUSEUM OF HISTORY

Most communities, as they grow and thrive, face the need for a place to house an increasing number of thieves and rabble-rousers who follow the progress. Fernandina was no different. By 1878, local authorities set out to construct a simple, sturdy jail on South 3rd Street. It was a one-story, rectangular building, equipped with appropriate iron cells and a room for jailers.

In 1935, the Nassau County commissioners authorized enlarging the county jail facility to provide more space by adding a second floor and sheathing the building in brick. Its design, popular in the 1930's, was done in what is called Art Modern architecture. Art Modern is noted for flat roofs, smooth facades and cubic shapes. The jail was dressed with multiple, extended brick at the roof line, glass blocks above the portico, and decorative concrete reliefs at the entrance.

Youngblood and Higginbotham were two names most heavily associated with this institution over the years though a number of sheriffs served Nassau County from here. A central county detention center was opened in Yulee in 1975 and this South 3rd Street facility was closed.

Shortly after its closing, seeds were planted to revive the old jail building by the Duncan Lamont Clinch Historical Society, with dreams of a museum to preserve artifacts of Amelia Island's past. The building was actually acquired in 1979. It emerged as the Fernandina Historical Museum, later the Florida Museum of Transportation and History, then the Eight Flags Museum of Nassau County.

Artifacts were collected and stored in the old cells and offices but it took until 1985 before the effort would actually get off the ground. The old hulk of the jail building was stripped of lathe and plaster to bare brick walls and by April of 1986, after thousands of volunteer man hours, the door was opened to the public and Florida's first oral history museum came to be.

In 1986, the museum was reorganized as the Amelia Island Museum of History (AIMH) and today is a model of organization and a leader in community involvement.

The Amelia Island Museum of History.

A relief sculpture on the South 3rd Street facade.

The nostalgic memorabilia comes to life in the museum. The windows retain the jail's steel bars, reminders of the past and security for the present. The "keepers of the past" have done a superb job with their restoration.

The Victorian Room.

The first floor exhibit hall authenticated down to a simulation of the Fernandina piers, dozens of large photographic murals, and a fascinating shrimp boat exhibit.

Hat and high-top shoes, perhaps purchased at the Prescott Shoe Store and Haberdashery.

With most of the history of Amelia Island based on maritime experiences, exhibits such as this compensating binnacle (a compass) follow that trend. In the background of the exhibit can be seen wood strips imbedded in mortar between the brick, strips used to secure the lathe strips and plastered walls in place.

The original old lock and key still secures the front set of bars, preventing unwanted after-hours intruders, before preventing unwanted escapes.

One can almost visualize Effingham Bailey cycling down South 7th Street on his pennyfarthing bicycle.

OLD SCHOOLHOUSE NO.1

In the mid-1880 to 1890 time period, significant development was beginning to take place east of 8th and Centre Streets. Houses were going up and available lots on Centre Street were at a premium. The county school board secured the property at the corner of Atlantic Avenue and 10th Street and hired architect Robert Schuyler to design and contractors James McGiffin and George Chase to build a schoolhouse.

A cornerstone was laid in April of 1886 with construction completed the same year. The original masonry vernacular building was 60 feet wide and 40 feet deep and had two large classrooms on each floor.

Its design has influences of the Italianate architectural style, using corbeled brick cornice, brick pilasters, round arch windows and entrances, and a belfry. In restoration, the belfry was scaled down in size to better conform to the size of the building.

Several years after the 1886 construction, an addition was added to the rear of the building.

The school served the community for 41 years before its last class graduated in 1927. By January of 1928, students moved into the new, larger school across Atlantic Avenue. After several years of abandonment, the building was purchased and used by the local Masonic Lodge.

Today, School House No. 1 survives, beautifully restored and maintained as commercial office space.

Medallion button of the front entrance doors.

Round arches are flush with brick walls on all doors and windows.

The simple main entrance with a circular transom above. Though not original to the building, it serves the restoration well.

The old school was used by a number of organizations over the years, for a variety of reasons. It retained its two classrooms down, and two classrooms up, for many years but economics would change all of that. The old school house has seen several restorations or renovations in the past 30 years. The first converted the two classrooms to smaller offices, each with entrances off of the hallway running along the east wall of the building. The entry hall and stairways were changed somewhat but are essentially of the old design. In the late 1990's, the old school received a make-over, refining previous restorations to better conform to period architecture.

The old balusters, hand rails, and newel posts are the originals, removed of dirt, chewing gum, et cetera, and restored to period.

Schoolroom window with a high transom for light and ventilation.

ST. JOSEPH'S ACADEMY

Later Changed to
St. Michael's Academy
Original site of
The Convent of the Sisters of St. Joseph

Buildings of the St. Joseph's Academy complex were built of brick, all shipped by schooner from Philadelphia, one ship load free of freight costs. The building to the right, originally one level, was given a second story in the mid-1880's. The chapel, completed in 1884, is at the far left.

As an institution, St. Joseph's Academy was completed and opened in 1882. The Sisters of St. Joseph moved into the third floor, the floor within the mansard roof. Students of all faiths were offered academic courses in both English and French with tuition, food, laundry, bed and bedding offered for $40.50 per quarter. A student received music lessons, including the use of the instrument, for $12.

Funding to build St. Joseph's Academy came to the Sisters of St. Joseph and the Catholic Church from donations, the sale of jams and jellies, the making and sale of lace, and a gift from the Mother House in Le Puy, France. The St. Joseph's order was instituted in Le Puy in 1648. The nuns on Amelia Island were associated with Le Puy until 1900.

In 1961, the Sisters of St. Joseph sold the academy to St. Michael's parish. Subsequently the name of the school changed to St. Michael's Academy. St. Michael's school operated until 1972 when its doors were closed.

A major restoration of all of the academy's buildings was initiated in 1997. St. Michael's Academy reopened in 1998 with preschool, adding kindergarten through fourth grades in 1999, and fifth through seventh grades in 2002. The third floor, or mansard level, which had been the residence of the nuns for many years, had been removed in 1960 for reasons of economy of maintenance. In the restoration process, the third floor was restored.

The three-story main structure of the Convent of the Sisters of St. Joseph, or St. Joseph's Academy, is one of the few examples of major Second Empire influence in Fernandina. Its defining feature is its mansard roof, double pitched with dormers.

Heavily embellished reliefs on the doors of the North 4th Street main entrance.

The transom above the North 4th Street entrance.

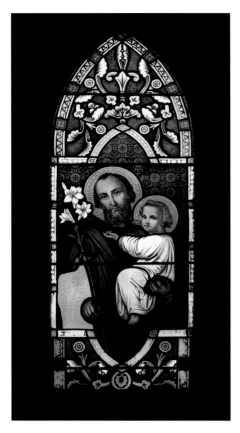

Stained glass above the balcony on the chapel's east wall.

Pine floors, newel posts and staircases have been immaculately restored to their 19th century beauty.

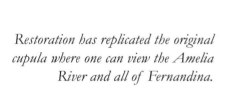

Restoration has replicated the original cupula where one can view the Amelia River and all of Fernandina.

One of fourteen stained glass windows that adorn the nave of the Sisters of St. Joseph chapel.

A painting of the chapel of the Sisters of St. Joseph, by Anni Mollerof, depicting the chapel as it appeared in its earliest days. The magnificent wall and ceiling frescoes remain but are hidden beneath layers of paint. The chapel today is used as a classroom, but the alter, with its many Christian adornments, remain for any future restorations. Stained-glass windows on either side of the altar were taken to the Cathedral of St. Augustine with the school's closure in 1972. They were replaced with solid-colored glass.

St. Joseph's Academy Collection

113

FIRST BAPTIST CHURCH

The First Baptist Church was organized in 1859 with its sanctuary at North 5th and Calhoun Streets. That building burned to the ground in 1887. The next year construction began on a replacement taking until the early 1890's to complete. It was a wood-frame building that went up at North 5th and Alachua Streets.

By 1926, with an ever-expanding congregation, and apparently no way to expand the wood frame church building, the old structure was razed and replaced with a much

Extensive remodeling to the sanctuary in 1976 enabled seating for the entire congregation.

larger brick neoclassic revival design very popular in that period. The building's architectural features are its colossal portico with flanking turrets, a brick pediment surrounded by dental moulding, ornate brickwork, and the circular seating arrangement of the sanctuary. Major additions were added to the building in 1952 and 1963 and extensive remodeling was accomplished in 1976. The two story educational building had been added in 1963.

A meeting of Colonial and Queen Anne.

FIRST MISSIONARY BAPTIST CHURCH

The First Missionary Baptist Church had its beginnings in 1860 when a group was organized under Elder William Rose as Pastor. The present site was purchased in 1873, construction of the present structure being completed in 1874. It stands today as the oldest African American Baptist church in continuous service as a place of worship in Florida.

Architecturally, the building is of Gothic Revival design. It is significant for its cross-gabled tower, its pedimental entrance, and its steep-gabled arch

The original steeple was damaged beyond repair in 1958 and removed. In the mid-1990's, a Federal grant made it possible to replace the spire that had been constructed there more than 120 years before.

The Emma B. Delaney educational building was completed in 1979, honoring this parishioner and her 20 years of missionary work in Liberia.

The sanctuary ceiling is a maze of dark-stained heart pine.

The sanctuary windows are of Rainbow-hued stained-glass Queen Anne era impression.

115

*The original clear glass windows were
replaced with leaded glass windows in 1926.*

FIRST
PRESBYTERIAN
CHURCH

One of the few antebellum structures still standing in Fernandina, the First Presbyterian Church is the oldest church building on Amelia Island and one of the oldest in Florida. It was constructed in 1858 in the Classic Revival tradition or New England Meeting House Style. The building sits on two lots, one donated by David Yulee, the other acquired from the Florida Railroad Company for $200. The building exterior is painted white clapboard with a tin roof above and a square belfry.

Within the sanctuary the floor is carpeted protecting the original yellow pine timbers. The ceiling is yellow pine milled in tongue-and-groove and crafted in triangular shapes that reflect a warm tone of light throughout. The stained-glass windows were installed in 1926, replacing the original clear glass. The organ was installed with a multitude of pipes hanging from the west chancel wall. The chancel arch is symbolically supported on either side by two columns with Roman Doric capitals powerful in design.

Services have been held within the sanctuary of the First Presbyterian Church for more than 140 years, interrupted only by Union forces that were garrisoned there during the War Between the States.

The single bay entrance porch is embellished with balustrade, columns, dental moldings, and a gabled pediment.

An array of pipes above the altar.

The Macedonia AME Church was organized in 1870 after a Samuel Irving arrived from Philadelphia and organized a prayer group in the name of the African Methodist Episcopal (AME) Church. These were the dark days for African Americans recently released from their bonds just a few years before.

In September of 2000, Macedonia A.M.E. began a major interior and exterior renovation that took 8 months to complete. The interior was gutted, new floors were laid, pews cleaned, polished, and cushions added, and a new heating and air conditioning system installed. The stained glass windows were removed, repaired, cleaned, and new frames added before reinstallation. Brass chandeliers were then added to the sanctuary.

MACEDONIA AME CHURCH

The beautifully restored sanctuary following recent renovations.

MEMORIAL UNITED METHODIST CHURCH

The first known Methodist Church building on Amelia Island was erected in 1870 at Broome and 6th Street. It served the church until 1926 when land donated by Effingham Bailey and John W. Simmons was accepted by the congregation to build a larger structure at 601 Centre Street. Begun in 1926 by contractor John Mann, its total construction was not completed until 1951.

The exterior design is neoclassic revival architecture with a colossal portico with Ionic columns, brick pilasters, tall arched windows, and a gabled roof with triangle parapets. Additions to the church were completed in 1951 and 1970.

The memorial chapel contains the altar and chapel railings of the old Kings Ferry Methodist Church, pews from the original Broome Street church, an old baptismal font, and an original Enoch Wood bust of John Wesley.

Massive memorial windows.

Sanctuary of the 1926 building.

NEW ZION MISSIONARY BAPTIST CHURCH

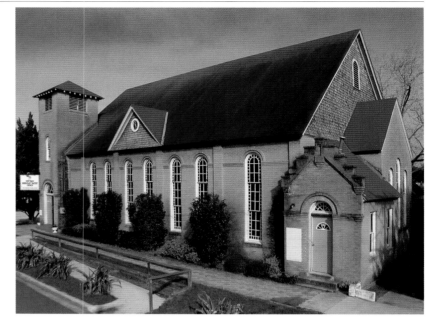

The barrel arch.

The New Zion Missionary Baptist Church was founded in May of 1870 as the second oldest African American missionary Baptist church on Amelia Island. The church was established under Rev. Lewis Cook and his followers who broke from the First Missionary Baptist Church. They constructed a wood frame building at 10th Street and Atlantic Avenue but in 1904 was destroyed by fire. The present building is a masonry vernacular design, constructed by William Rivers, an African American Fernandina contractor.

One of seventeen.

The large stained glass windows emit a feeling of warmth, enhanced by the open beamed trusses, unique in its barrel-arch design. The ceiling is stained pine tongue and groove.

Early St. Michael's Catholic Church.

ST. MICHAEL'S CATHOLIC CHURCH

Catholicism planted its roots on Amelia many years before St.Michael's sanctuary was built, brought first by the Spanish, remaining through the British period, and strengthening during the second Spanish period. There was a mission on the bluff at Old Town for a time pastored by Father Emile Hillaire. Father Hillaire was appointed by Bishop Verot, the Apostolic Vicar of Florida.

In 1859, a wood church was constructed in new Fernandina on the present site of St. Michael's. When Union troops took over Fernandina in 1862, Father Henry Peter Clavruel was priest of the small congregation.

In 1869, the first permanent priest came to the church from Italy. Father Carolus Sartorio, 26 years old, died suddenly a year later. He was succeeded by Father John Bertazzi, who oversaw construction of the new brick sanctuary in 1872. Under Father Betazzi's guidance, the first two nuns, Sisters of St. Joseph, arrived to prepare the parish's children for their first communion.

The church, one of the first brick structures in Fernandina, is designed in the Mission or Moorish architectural style.

The brick exterior was stuccoed in 1936 and the stained-glass windows were added in the same decade.

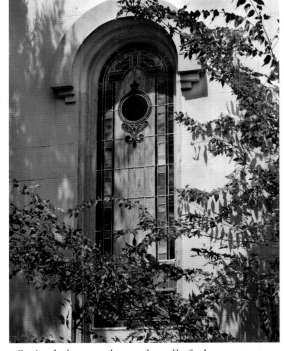

Stained glass on the south wall of the sanctuary.

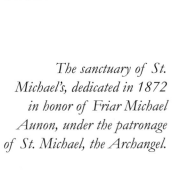

The sanctuary of St. Michael's, dedicated in 1872 in honor of Friar Michael Aunon, under the patronage of St. Michael, the Archangel.

Sometime after the Civil War, the first Trinity Methodist Church building was constructed just to the west of the present Trinity Church. A new building was constructed from 1891 to 1893 at the intersection of 8th and Ash Streets..

The brick vernacular design highlights its lancet arched windows, brick corbeling and pilasters, and its three-story bell tower.

In the late 1990's, Trinity and a community group organized as "Friends of Trinity" raised $350,000 to assist in a major restoration effort of the historic structure. Stained glass was removed, cleaned and re-leaded. The sanctuary within was refurbished, brick walls of the exterior experienced a face lift, and the bell tower experienced major structural renovations.

Original brass fixtures hang from the ceiling and exposed ceiling trusses, long ago converted from gas to electric. Pews are curved to face the center of the chancel, somewhat unusual for church furniture of its time.

The stained-glass windows of Trinity were purchased in England and total 26 in number.

TRINITY UNITED METHODIST CHURCH

The rose window of the south wall.

Lancet windows beneath the west gable.

ST. PETER'S EPISCOPAL CHURCH

The magnificent structure of St. Peter's Episcopal Church epitomizes Gothic architecture in small town America. Its massive and buttressed walls, its stained-glass windows that depict the community's history, and its sanctuary all emit an air of a church of Medieval times.

The tract now occupied by the sanctuary of St. Peters Episcopal Church was deeded in 1878 by Samuel A. Swann to the Reverend John Freeman Young. Designed by Robert S. Schuyler, St. Peter's Episcopal Church was constructed from 1881 through 1884 by contractor George Chase. The first service took place on Good Friday of 1884.

Eight years later, St. Peters experienced a disastrous fire that destroyed most of the sanctuary and tower interior. The original windows and furniture were destroyed in the holocaust. Later, the windows were replaced and most of the furniture restored by the original craftsman. During the restoration of the 1890's, modifications to the design changed the tower's appearance, added a grand entrance on the southwest corner, and added 7 feet to the east end. Unfortunately, in the restoration process, architect Robert Schuyler fell from the tower's high scaffolding, never fully recovering from his injuries.

Today St. Peter's Episcopal Church is the finest example of Gothic Revival architecture in Florida. Its design features a steeply-pitched roof, lancet windows, and a tower with a castellated parapet. Its 18-inch thick walls are made of tabby overlaid with cement. The bare tabby walls visible within the tower still encase non-supporting charcoaled timbers from the fire of 1892.

There were 17 original stained-glass windows with several added in the mid-20th century. All highlight the history and people of Fernandina down through the years.

The nave is warm in dark tones of heart-pine pews and an open timber ceiling designed in the pattern of an inverted ship's hull. The pews were crafted in Gainesville, Florida at a cost of $6.50 each.

The organ was purchased in 1893, after the fire, at a cost of $2,000. The cathedral-style instrument includes 839 pipes, many of which are beautifully embellished. The organ casing was designed by the building's architect, Robert Schuyler, and meticulously crafted of Florida pine and cedar by Robert M. Henderson, a church member and local coffin maker. The Organ Historical Society states that the organ "is a stellar and perhaps singular example of the best organs built in any age in this country..." It is truly a remarkable piece of work.

No matter the time of day, light falls into the sanctuary, enriching the Gothic furnishings, its columns, arches, and trappings.

St. Peter's stained-glass windows were constructed in New York by Edward Colgate with the exception of the Doctor's Window crafted by W.J. McPherson of Boston. Seventeen stained-glass windows were installed in the original construction, all replaced or repaired following the 1892 fire.

The Sacristy is in the south transept where stained-glass windows known as cherub windows can be found (center).

Peering through the chancel arch to the north transept and the 120-year-old pipe organ.

The original old church bell perched high atop the tower, as always, still sounds fifteen minutes prior to church services.

The fountain on the south wall of the Dungeness Tabby House is replicated on a garden area wall at the Greyfield Inn. It symbolizes the stature of a closely-knit family and an era of elegance.

The roads of Cumberland Island are just wide enough to accommodate one vehicle and meander for long stretches through the oak forests and dense underbrush from one plantation site to another. They track through areas that were once immense sea island cotton fields, orange orchards, and stands of large pine and hickory, long since abandoned and reverted back to the wild. An 1898 map shows the road north from Dungeness as Stafford Road joining with others such as Pratts, Andrews, Hickory Hill, Holly Field, and eventually Plum Orchard Road. Wild deer, horses and formerly domestic hogs are seen crossing from one grazing ground to another. In the distance (above) two hogs can be seen and just beyond, and barely visible, is a young fawn.

124

CUMBERLAND *Island* Georgia

Sprinkled amongst oak and pine forests at the edge of broad marshlands are a few historic monuments of the 19th and early 20th century that live on, preserved in time. The grounds are vestiges of British colonial rule, of grand and elegant life-style, simple folk, cotton fields, and slavery.

Its history is awash with names such as British General and founding Governor of Georgia James Oglethorpe, wealthy planter Robert Stafford, Revolutionary War Major-General Nathanael Greene, Light-horse Harry Lee (the father of General Robert E. Lee), and member of the famed steel industry family of Pittsburgh, Thomas Carnegie. Today, the name Cumberland Island conjures thoughts and memories of the Carnegie family, as time has diminished the memory of many earlier names. Except for the privately-owned original old Stafford House, the grand old homes of Cumberland were built by and for the Carnegies.

History here, however, began hundreds of years before the arrival of Thomas and Lucy Coleman Carnegie. In the 16th century, the Spanish occupied the island, established a mission and a nearby fort in their defense against the French. Both the island and fort were called San Pedro.

Following the Spanish departure from the island, and the British establishment of the colony of Georgia in 1733, General

Greyfield Inn Landing.

James Oglethorpe came to San Pedro, where he erected Fort Saint Andrews on the north end of the island near the settlement of Barrimacke, and Fort Prince William on the south end of the island. Lore has it that he renamed San Pedro as Cumberland Island, after the Duke of Cumberland of Kent, England.

By the 1750's, the English were issuing land grants to those residents established on the island. In the succeeding years, a substantial number of homes were erected, one of them said to be Oglethorpe's on the south end near his Fort Prince William. One writer of note reported that he called his lodge "Dungeness" after a country home belonging to the Duke of Cumberland. This would establish the "first" Dungeness of the island.

In the years surrounding the American Revolution, the island was nearly deserted, save the Thomas Lynch plantation on the north end. Others such as John H. McIntosh, Jacob Weed, Alen Thomas, Robert and Thomas Stafford, John Houston, and Henry Osborne owned property there, but it is questionable as to the locations of these homes. The British, from time to time, anchored in the surrounding waters and used the island to forage for beef, wood, and fresh water.

In 1783, Revolutionary War hero Nathanael Greene signed an indenture purchasing half interest in nine plantations on Cumberland Island ostensibly to engage in the timber business. One writer noted that he paid 5,000 British pounds while another believed it to be worth 40,000 pounds. Greene's rice plantation at Savannah were not producing as he had expected. In financial straights, he soon entered into negotiations to sell portions of his properties to settle his many debts, primarily those incurred purchasing provisions for his war-era troops. General Greene, his wife Catherine, and their children had been living at Mulberry Grove, their Savannah home, in the early-1780's, with Nathanael making frequent visits south to Cumberland.

The early to mid-1780's were unstable years for the Florida/Georgia border area, including Cumberland Island. While in Savannah, Greene received information that several hundred intruders from Florida were on Cumberland Island cutting large quantities of timber and shipping it off. Several months later, a Spanish paper confirmed that American vessels were carrying off large amounts of timber. His plea to the Governor of Georgia was in vain as troops could not be sent. The problem eventually subsided with the loss of large quantities of timber.

Although Greene had great expectations for the island, he never permanently moved his family to Cumberland. Greene and Catherine remained at their Savannah estate for several more years. Unexpectedly, on June 19, 1786, Nathanael Greene died from a severe case of sunstroke, leaving his wife and five children with heavy debt.

The Tabby House is believed the oldest structure on Cumberland Island, built in 1800 during the construction of Nathanael Greene's Dungeness. It served as the house for the gardeners, connected to the main house by a high wall.

Dormer windows were the only source of outside light to the second floor.

When the cottage was converted to an office by Lucy Carnegie, the second floor was removed and replaced with large pine cabinets which stored the immense amount of paperwork generated by the estate. The estate at one time, covered 90% of Cumberland Island.

THE GREENE - MILLER
DUNGENESS

A year before his death, the Greenes had hired Phineas Miller, a Yale graduate of the highest caliber, to tutor their children. Miller soon found himself involved in the financial affairs of the family, and was said to be very competent.

Over the next ten years, Phineas drew very close to the family and to Catherine. In 1796, still living at Mulberry Grove, Phineas and Catherine married. In April of 1799, the Millers moved permanently to Cumberland Island. Their plans included building the house that Nathanael had envisioned, but for a time they lived in a house of unknown location.

By 1802, a number of improvements had been made to the island including a network of roads and a dam north of Plum Orchard believed constructed to improve irrigation in cotton fields of that area. Phineas had visions of the lush land beneath their feet providing a wealth in healthy crops. However, Phineas' dreams were short-lived. Miller died in 1803.

A relative of Catherine's, Ray Sands, came the island in 1798. It is speculated that he was overseeing the construction of a new Dungeness for Phineas and Catherine. Phineas himself had designed a magnificent mansion. Upon Phineas' death, Sands assumed management of much of Catherine's affairs, and saw to the completion of this second Dungeness.

According to legend, the new estate intentionally included several unfinished rooms. Apparently there was a superstition in the family that if the house was ever fully completed, a misfortune would occur.

Many years later, Harper's Magazine described this great mansion "built of concrete... or tabby as the natives less elegantly name it. The house stood on an artificial mound, was four stories high, and contained forty rooms. The exterior was stuccoed about the first story, the facade was adorned with six stoned pilasters rising to the eaves, and the entrance, faced with hewn granite, was approached by a flight of massive steps. The four towering chimneys suggest the comfort and good cheer for which Dungeness was celebrated when Mr. and Mrs. Miller there dispensed a liberal hospitality.... The place is so full of sentiment, of old-world romance and beauty, that one can hardly believe that what he is gazing on can be in the United States."

With the death of Catherine Greene Miller around 1814, her daughter, Louisa Greene Shaw, inherited all of Dungeness plantation and assumed the position of mistress of Dungeness. During the Louisa Shaw period at Dungeness, or until about 1831, the island remained largely a wilderness with a small number of families. With Louisa's knowledge of horticulture and management skills, Dungeness prospered beyond the imagination of her father. With Louisa's death in 1831, Dungeness and Oakland Plantations were passed to her nephew, Phineas Miller Nightingale, and the estate entered into the family's third generation.

During the early years of Nightingale's ownership of Dungeness, the estate was prosperous from sea-island cotton, oranges, corn, sweet potatoes, and olives. Large stands of oak were cut and sold to make way for larger planting fields. Though initially Nightingale's Dungeness was still referred to as a "superb mansion," in little more than 10 years it was said "going to ruin." Phineas continued, however, in Catherine Miller and Louisa Shaw's social tradition, entertaining visitors and attracting friend and family weddings. In 1839, Nightingale advertised the sale of a plantation on Cumberland Island. By late 1843, 1,200 acres of Oakland and its slaves were sold at auction to one of his neighbors, Robert Stafford, Jr. Nightingale's fortunes declined and his tenure at Dungeness ended by 1860.

Other plantation owners on the island prospered. Robert Stafford, Jr. purchased a great deal of the old Greene properties in the late 1830's and, approaching the Civil War, he owned some 8,000 acres of land and had, by far, the most slaves. During the war, Union occupation led to a what was termed an accidental burning of the Dungeness mansion.

The Nathanael Greene Dungeness stood four stories high, a massive monument to this hero of the Revolutionary War. Unfortunately, Greene died before Dungeness's completion and future financial successes of its farming operations. Union occupation of the island, and their encampment at the Greene - Miller Dungeness, led to carelessness and the accidental burning of Dungeness mansion.

Historic American Building Survey - National Park Service.

THE CARNEGIE
DUNGENESS

The third home of the same name.

Thomas Morrison Carnegie was but five years of age when he came to America with his parents, William and Margaret, and his older brother, Andrew, from their native Dunfermline, Fifeshire, Scotland. The year was 1848. They settled in Pittsburgh where William labored in a cotton mill and Margaret cobbled shoes. About 1859, Thomas quit school and took work with the Pennsylvania Railroad as a telegrapher, then went to work for his brother as his personal secretary.

In the mid-1850's, Thomas had taken an interest in Lucy Coleman, daughter of a wealthy industrialist. It would be after the Civil War and a flirting relationship between Andrew and Lucy, that Thomas and Lucy would join hands in marriage in June of 1866.

Thomas Carnegie's climb to fame in the world of steel began in the late 1850's and climaxed only with his death in 1886. His career would always be under the shadow of his older brother, Andrew, but it is said that Thomas had the creativity and motivation that built the Carnegie empire. By 1881, a number of Carnegie-owned ore mines, furnaces, and mills consolidated as Carnegie Brothers & Company, Ltd., with Thomas being appointed Chairman of the Board.

In the early 1880's, Thomas and his wife, Lucy Coleman Carnegie, sailed south from their winter home at Jekyll Island, along the coast of Georgia, where Lucy found the secluded and beautiful Cumberland Island and concluded that it should be hers. Lucy was somewhat familiar with the area, having attended a boarding school in Fernandina as a young girl.

The first land purchase was on November 17, 1881, when Thomas acquired 4,000 acres of the old Greene-Miller estate known as Dungeness that included houses, outbuildings, stables, orange and olive groves, and gardens. This land was more recently a part of Stafford Plantation. Carnegie paid $35,000. The following spring, he acquired another 8,240 acres from heirs of Robert Stafford, in partnership with a Pittsburgh associate, for $40,000.

Thomas wasted little time making plans and beginning a transformation of the old Dungeness property. He had the remains of the Greene/Miller Dungeness razed sometime in 1882, retaining and restoring lawns, gardens, and walkways. He made a concerted effort to retain the old estate's historical and aesthetic significance, retaining

The first Carnegie Dungeness built by Thomas and Lucy Carnegie in the early to mid-1880's was the epitome of Queen Anne style, designed by Andrew Peebles of Pittsburgh and constructed by McKenzie &Patterson of Boston.

National Park Service - Cumberland Island National Seashore, St. Marys, GA.

National Park Service - Cumberland Island National Seashore, St. Marys, GA.

After the passing of Thomas, Lucy Carnegie expanded Dungeness to accommodate her children and her many visiting friends. These additions, in the 1890's, were contracted to the architectural firm of Peabody & Stearns of Boston.

128

the old Tabby House and Greene-Miller cemetery.

The cornerstone of Thomas' new Dungeness was laid March 26, 1884, with all pomp and ceremony. It took about a year for the contractors to build the magnificent Queen Anne mansion, 120 by 56 feet, three stories in height, and a tower 100 feet to its peak. Its facade was covered with granite, and topped with Vermont slate roofs on the verandas, dormers, and belvederes. Within was a 25- by 55-foot grand hall, with ceilings at 16 feet except over the grand fireplace area which stood 26 feet in height. Within the hall were three ten foot high stained-glass windows that illuminated the entire hall.

There was an 18- by 24-foot parlor, an equal size dining room, a gun room, kitchen, scullery, and so on. The second floor held the living apartments of the family, guest rooms, and a library. The attic had six sleeping rooms, presumably for overflow visitors or children.

The cost of Carnegie's new Dungeness was $285,000, nearly $5 million in today's money. The new Dungeness afforded them a luxurious life for the next year. They would be back and forth between their Pittsburgh interests and their new home on Cumberland Island.

While at Homewood, his Pittsburgh home, Thomas contracted a cold which developed into pneumonia. He died unexpectedly. The year was 1886 and he was but forty three years of age. Lucy was left with nine children, a loving heart for her children and family, and a massive estate.

The land partnership with Thomas' associate concluded the year of Thomas' death. The following year Lucy acquired the deed of the old Stafford estate giving her some 12,240 acres on the island. Lucy began adding to the main house and assuming complete control of her lands. It is said that "she was responsible for creating a feudal fiefdom on the island that was self sufficient in almost every respect. From this mansion, Lucy Carnegie supervised her estate like a feudal lord over her principality."

By 1899, six of Lucy's children had come of age, a trust giving them the old Stafford estate. No doubt through a prearranged agreement, they signed the property back over to their mother, who by then owned 90 per cent of Cumberland Island. Apparently the family agreement or understanding was that each would receive their due in one form or another.

The Stafford house was given to William Coleman Carnegie and his wife, Martha Gertrude Ely. This was a wood frame structure and was richly furnished in library, parlor, drawing rooms and bedrooms throughout the second floor. On January 5, 1900, the Stafford House was completely gutted by fire at a loss estimated between $60 and $75,000. Lucy had a replacement house constructed very much like the house that was destroyed, with William as his own architect.

As her children grew and married, Lucy acquired more land and built five very substantial homes for her children between the years 1893 and 1903: Plum Orchard, Greyfield, the Cottage, the Pool House (the Casino), and the Grange. Two of these, Plum Orchard and Greyfield, are featured in succeeding pages and so are not elaborated on here.

The first that she had built was the "Cottage"

not far from the main house, for her son Thomas Morrison Carnegie, Jr. It was begun before his father's death but finished years later. This was a frame structure with upper and lower porches on two sides appearing like an old plantation house of the deep South. The front facade was columned with Ionic capitals on the second story and Doric below. This cottage was destroyed by fire in the 1940's and never replaced.

The Pool house was built about 1900 and is also known as the Casino or recreation and guest house. It was designed by New York architect John Ingle and constructed by local contractor, James McGiffin. This building was 150 feet long and housed a large swimming pool, a gymnasium, a billiard room, and an apartment for Frank Carnegie. It is now in ruins located several hundred feet east of the main Dungeness house.

The Grange, just east of the pool house ruins, was built in 1903 for William E. Page who was hired in 1891 to administer the Carnegie homes and facilities on Cumberland Island. It is still inhabited today.

Lucy Coleman Carnegie died January 16, 1916, at the age of sixty-nine and was buried in the Carnegie cemetery near Dungeness. The Dungeness estate was inherited by her surviving children, five sons and three daughters, with a trust set up to maintain the 16,000 acres for their benefit.

Finding that the Dungeness mansion was too costly to maintain, it was vacated in 1925 and there began the doom of the third Dungeness. For many years the stately old mansion was exposed to the elements without repairs or maintenance. By the 1950's, the house was said to be of little value, but thought to have been symbolic of the family wealth.

Beginning about 1956, conflicts between the family and poachers took a turn for the worse. By May of 1959, a gamekeeper shot at an illegal hunter which began a series of events that culminated with the burning of the great Dungeness mansion on June 24th. The obvious conclusion was that it was set afire by arsonists in revenge of the family's intolerance of mainland poachers. The ruins remain but the Carnegie Dungeness has passed.

The mysterious burning of the Carnegie Dungeness began at about 6 P.M. and burned until after midnight. The charred remnants of Dungeness remain today much as they were in the days following the great fire.

National Park Service - St. Marys Museum Archives

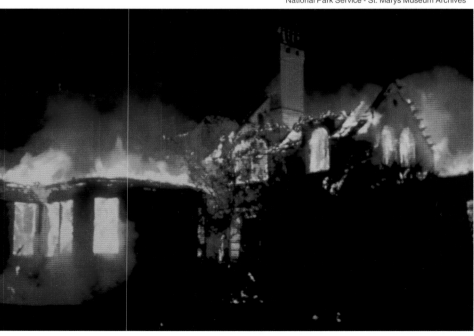

THE RUINS OF CARNEGIE'S DUNGENESS

The west wing.

The Pool house, fallen to shambles in just the last three decades.

A look within the remains of the two floors of the west wing.

The ivy cover pergola stretched from the tabby house west to the Cottage and offered good sun protection during the hot summer months. Just to the south of this central arch were the sprawling gardens of Dungeness.

Looking to the northwest over the main house, and below right, the southwest corner.

A look through the main gates from the old Stafford Road.

The west wing.

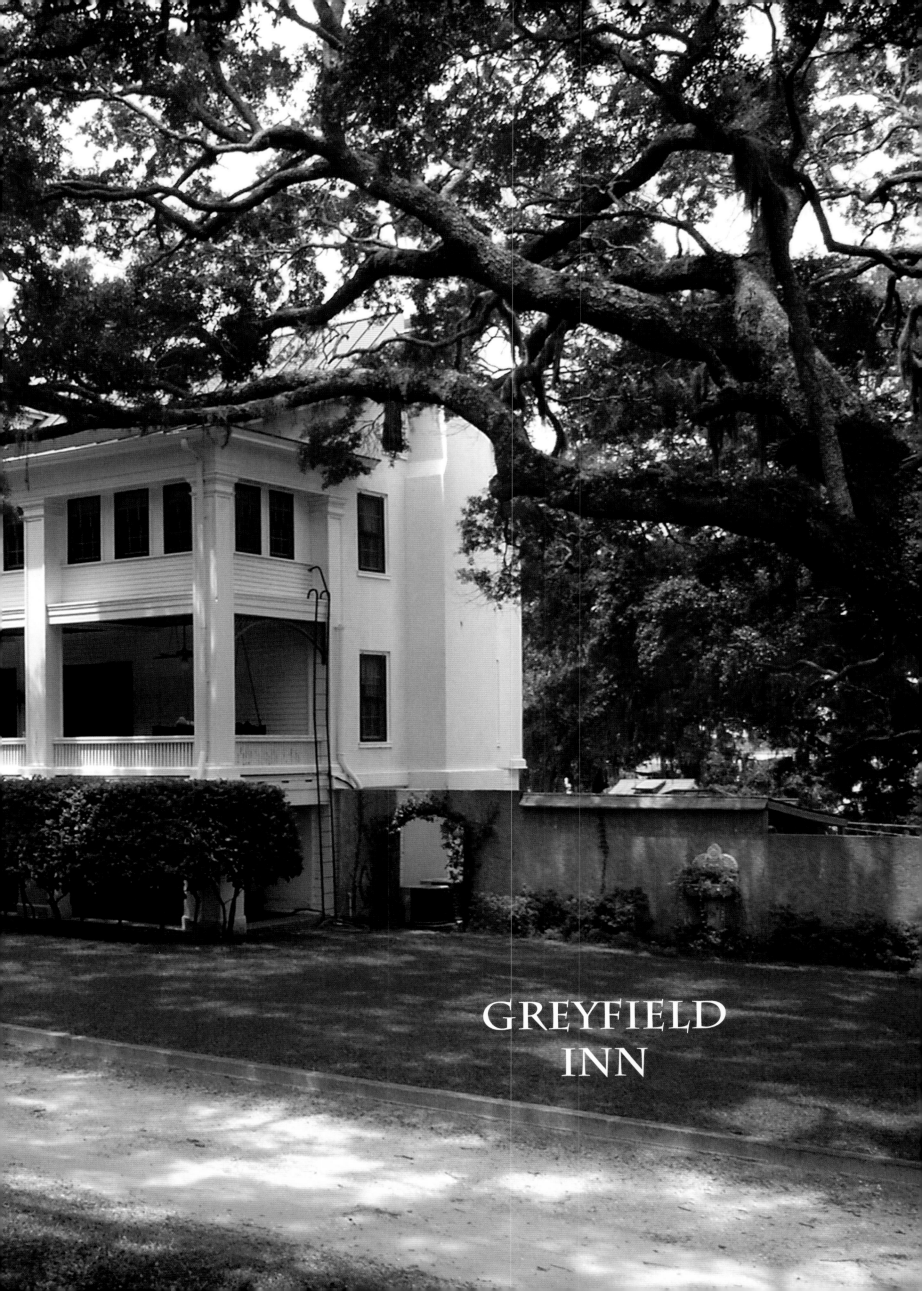

GREYFIELD
INN

GREYFIELD INN

The Greyfield home was built by Lucy Carnegie in 1900 as a wedding gift for her daughter, Margaret "Retta" Carnegie, who married Oliver Garrison Ricketson. The home was later passed to their daughter, Lucy, who married Robert Ferguson. It remained Lucy's home until 1962 when Greyfield became an inn operated by the family.

The home is spacious with three levels and an attic, and a veranda that runs the width of the second floor. The third floor originally had a matching veranda which was enclosed in Lucy Ferguson's time and converted to bedroom space for her children and guests.

Greyfield continues on today as a grand and graceful mansion inn, in a peaceful and relaxing environment. Carnegie descendents have retained ownership and provide day trips and overnight accommodations for those wishing to visit this historic estate.

A large living room on the south end of the house has windows on three sides. There is a central fireplace and the ever-present bench in front of the hearth which seems were found in all of the Carnegie houses.

On the east wall is a wedding portrait of Lucy Ferguson, Rhetta and Oliver's daughter, and last family occupant of Greyfield. On the north wall is a library of fine books, part of the large collection found in the library down the hall. All of the furnishings at Greyfield are original to the house.

The Ricketson - Ferguson family library.

The entrance is from the right in the picture, where you pass the staircase to glimpse at the river in the rear. On one side is the old cloakroom, now a bar, and on the other side, the back staircase. The hall pictured below leads to the library and a first floor bedroom.

The front staircase to the rooms above and the kitchen and dining area below.

Indoor convenience at an early date.

*The old cannon sits
next to the remains
of the pergola.*

A luxury, expensive in its day.

Footprints on tile.

*The cannons that stick from the ground in the front yard are said to be
from Fort Clinch. They are inscribed "USA 1861." There is very little
that is new at Greyfield. Bath fixtures are as they were nearly a hundred
years ago and horses roam the entire island as they have done for hundreds
of years. Greyfield is like a trip back in time to when Lucy'Carnegie's
sons wore knickers and drove the island in their electric cars.*

One on each end of the house.

Photo by Patrick McLean

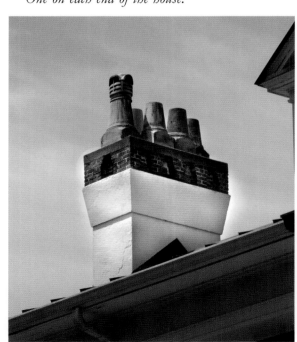

The attic rooms were apartments for maids and employees that worked in the house. They are now quaint little getaway rooms of the inn, sought after for their simple charm.

The dressing room looking through to Retta's bedroom.

On the second floor and overlooking the front yard was Retta's room. It connected to a dressing room (above) and to another bedroom behind. The apartment is roomy and comfortable with both morning and evening sun shining through ancient oaks. Down the hall were bedrooms of their children, Lucy and Oliver.

The west veranda with an extended porch is closest to the old plantation docks on the Brick Hill River, connecting to the inland waterway.

PLUM ORCHARD

No matter how you view Plum Orchard, the grand old Lady of Cumberland, there is a marvelously framed picture as if taken from a story book.

Largest and most elegant of the Carnegie estates was Plum Orchard, built by Lucy Carnegie in 1898 for her son George Lauder Carnegie and his wife Margaret Thaw. The house was constructed on the site of an older plantation owned by a Peter Bernardy who also called his plantation Plum Orchard. Its name is derived from a plum orchard that once grew on this spot more than 200 years ago. Bernardy is buried in a small plot nearby.

This was the fourth estate built as a part of the Carnegie holdings on Cumberland. First was Dungeness, then Greyfield, then the Cottage, then came Plum Orchard. Yet to be built was the Pool house for her bachelor sons and guests.

The house was designed in the Georgian Revival tradition, initially a rectangular building with hipped roof, a large two-story portico columned with Ionic capitals, topped with a monumental pediment. The house is built of brick covered with stucco, with wood joists and steel frames. It is large and solid. The front porch beneath the columns extends to the east and west wings with balustrade. In all of its years, the house has always been painted white. It's hard to imagine that it would be painted any other color.

Plum Orchard contains thirteen bedrooms, a dining room, study, music hall, gun room, and library. The east wing was added in 1906 with a swimming pool, squash court, and dressing rooms. The interior is finished in a variety of local and exotic woods. The entrance hall, staircase, and dining room are all oak with carved ornaments. The gun room is chestnut, the living room is sycamore, with most of the servant and bedrooms being yellow pine. The floors are quarter sawn yellow pine. Within the house you have the feeling of substantial, but when viewed from the outside you get the feeling of grandeur.

The house was occupied for many years by George and Margaret Carnegie. Though the couple was childless, they were very active in the family, always entertaining nieces, nephews, and siblings. There was always golf, hunting, and horseback riding through the thicket and out to the beach. George kept a large power boat out at the dock which occupied much of his time, entertaining family and friends when the weather was right. Margaret, the good housekeeper that she was, oversaw a staff that kept the house in immaculate condition.

George's death came in 1921 while in New York. That year Margaret went to Europe and the house was closed. She remarried there, returning with her French husband who insisted the furnishings be sent to New York and sold. The house was preserved, refurnished, and life went on at the Orchard.

The next occupants of Plum Orchard were Nancy Carnegie Johnston, George's sister, and her husband, Marius and their children. They lived there for many years, maintaining the estate until the early 1970's when the house was signed over to the National Park Service.

Column and pediment detail.

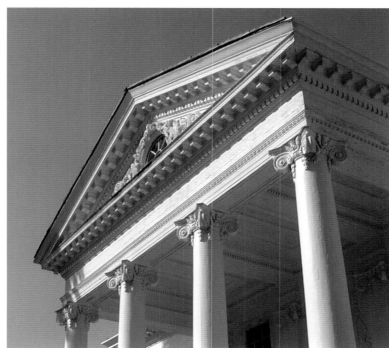

Entering the house from between the front veranda columns, guests were greeted in the lush reception hall. Richly stained oak moldings encircle a heavily embellished yet tasteful canvas wallpaper.

An Ionic pilaster symbolically supporting the entablature and detailed oak cornice moldings above.

The main staircase winds to the living area on the second floor. Tucked beneath the center landing is a niche or, more correctly, an inglenook . Here is the hearth and two pub-type benches where family and friends shared conversation over a sparkling fire.

The ship's bell hangs above the stairway and is reachable from the second floor hall that stretches the length of the house. It was used on special occasions to call guests to dinner, and by visiting children who loved to hear its sound. Inscribed on the bell is "Carnegie - Plum Orchard - October 1898.

The hallway leading from the entry hall to the west wing grand hall and steps that lead to several of the wing bedrooms.

The west wing great hall that was used for entertaining, music, and sitting in front of the fire. The far door enters onto the west wing veranda and beyond, the path to the docks.

Summer or winter, the pool was always accessible to the family members. One wonders why you would want to descend steps to such a depth.

Imagine household servants, weaving their way through Carnegie children playing on this spacious porch.

The china cupboard, spacious and detailed to keep fine china and polish prized silver.

A huge working kitchen where one can almost smell the fragrances of grand dinners of fresh game caught on the island.

AFRICAN BAPTIST CHURCH

Near the north end of Cumberland Island there is a small settlement at Half Moon Bluff, first inhabited in 1890 on five acres sold to Mason T. Burbank and five to Charles A. Miller. The 52 lots which resulted from those sales were purchased by Negroes, many of them former slaves. Out of the ashes of the American Civil War, many found a peaceful spot to call home and to build their own African Baptist Church. The little one-room log church, built in 1893, gave relief to the island's Negro suffering and poverty, and served as the settlement's schoolhouse and gathering center.

By 1937, recognizing that a new building was needed, members solicited the owner of the nearby hotel who donated lumber from an abandoned house. The church members themselves then constructed the one-room sanctuary that exists today. The building is a simple structure having seven windows, a double door entrance, and a metal roof added in recent years.

Architecturally, the building itself is not necessarily significant for there have been structures of this type throughout the South. What does make this small building meaningful is that its congregation was an offshoot of the Southern gatherings that began when George Liele, the first black Baptist in Georgia, began preaching to slaves on plantations along the Savannah River in Georgia. The First Baptist Church of Savannah evolved from that very first black church in America, as most likely did the small church on Cumberland.

Its place in history advanced over a hundred years later when, on September 21, 1996, much to the surprise of an entire nation, the famous son of President John F. Kennedy, Sr., John, Jr. wed Carolyn Bessette. It was a very private Roman Catholic ceremony in the primitive chapel. It is rumored that John had visited the secluded resort owned by the Carnegie friends of his parents during his early years.

The surrounding buildings now serve as a wildlife research center.

The Riverview, St. Mary's, Ga.

The Riverview Hotel

Postcards from the Jerry and Gaila Brandon collection.

EARLY DAYS OF ST. MARYS

Osborne Street

Postcards from the Jerry and Gaila Brandon collection.

The South Georgia community of St. Marys is steeped in 220 years of history. Its founders were early Camden County citizens who came from nearby Cumberland Island to a spot on the St. Marys River that was then called Buttermilk Bluff.

Jacob Weed was granted 1620 acres of land on the winding river, which he split amongst nineteen subscribers who each acquired four, 4-acre squares at $38 per square. Each of the nineteen investors agreed to build a house of logs, frame, or brick, on their four squares of four acres. That was November of 1787.

The name first given their town was St. Patrick, short-lived, as it was changed to St. Marys by 1792. The streets were platted with wide avenues which eventually would be shaded with massive oaks.

Harbor facilities, as crude as they may have been, were constructed and new blood began trickling into the fledgling community from all parts of the South, to what became the southeastern most port in the United States. Amelia Island and Florida, at that time, were still part of a Spanish colony.

In its first thirty years, St. Marys was a frontier town, populated with a mixture of merchants, innkeepers, drifters, and dock workers. Some came escaping Spanish rule to the south. Others were simply rowdy soldiers from the fort at nearby Point Peters.

Most of the original investors sold their interests and never made old Buttermilk Bluff their homes. Their original intent was to build a port to ship their goods grown on nearby Cumberland Island.

The War of 1812 brought a blockade of the coastal ports of the United States by British warships. It had little effect on St. Marys until, in 1815, one month after the Treaty of Ghant which formally ended the war, the British fleet entered Cumberland Sound. The large fleet split, anchoring at Cumberland Island, north in Kings Bay, and on the St. Marys River off of St. Marys. Cumberland was taken and landing parties were sent to St. Marys. Given the threat of burning the town to the ground, authorities capitulated in the face of overwhelming British forces. From Cumberland and St. Marys, the British were able to control the southern border and its river traffic.

After failing to acquire customs funds in the possession of Archibald Clark, Collector of the Port, a large force was sent up river on barges to destroy Clark's steam mill on Spanish Creek. Captain William Cone of the Georgia Militia, with a band of twenty-eight men, advanced ahead of the British and positioned themselves along the river bank, repeatedly firing volleys at the invaders, then withdrawing to the next vantage point and firing again. British losses were staggering with one-hundred and eighty British soldiers killed and an equal number wounded. Captain Cone's small force did not lose a single man and the mill was saved. The British retreated back to St. Marys and soon departed the area. That was the last time a large foreign force attacked the shores of the United States.

The years before the War Between the States were prosperous years for St. Marys, in contrast to Fernandina which was suffering the worst economic period of its history. At St. Marys, outlying plantations were thriving with industry and commerce rapidly expanding.

By 1848, a demographic on Georgia noted that St. Marys had five churches and nine dry goods and grocery stores, three schools, and a population of 627. St. Marys was a pleasant and healthy seaport.

When the Civil War and Union troops finally reached the shores of the St. Marys River the little seaport was ravaged and its citizens scattered to all parts of the interior. The year was 1862. Many of those who left never returned after the war. Those who did found destruction of most homes and businesses.

It took years for the broken town to recover, as it did with most small towns of the old South.

Turning into the 1870's, conditions improved dramatically and the population increased to more than 750. River traffic was again steaming in from Fernandina and on to Kings Ferry and Traders Hill. Mills went back into full operation, longleaf yellow pine was stacked everywhere, and tall-masted ships lined the harbor. New homes were going up as fast as labor would allow. The South was in recovery and so was St. Marys.

It would, however, continue to be a roller coaster ride for more than a hundred years. The Victorian era brought prosperity in marine related occupations and just into the 20th century the St. Marys and Kingsland Railroad opened a new highway to the outside world. A revolutionized shrimping industry brought new ships and processing plants, and until it ran out, yellow pine lumber was on every seagoing ship leaving the docks.

Through the 1930's, St. Marys and Camden County suffered along with the rest of the country with years of economic depression. In 1940, St. Marys was able to attract a Northerner, Isaac Gilman, who established and built the St. Marys Kraft paper processing mill which employed hundreds and put food back on the table of many who had endured those years of depression.

Today, the economy of St. Marys, and for hundreds of miles around, capitalize on the growth of southern or slash pine, with forests that grow the timber and mills that process the pulp into a wide variety of products.

Historic Kings Bay, the site of a British invasion in 1815, is now the home port of America's Trident nuclear submarines. Historic St. Marys is now a friendly tourist spot and gateway to the Cumberland Island National Seashore.

BACON - BURNS HOUSE

This was the home of local physician Dr. Henry Bacon, built in the 1830's, in a prospering St. Marys community. Though it isn't known who actually built this home, it is believed to have been Bacon, whose descendents sold to Irish-born Samuel Burns in 1871 for $1900.

Its design is of the Federal style with pine facade, central hall within, originally with two rooms over two rooms, and a detached kitchen to the rear. In this original section there are hand-pegged beams and Roman numerals chiseled in the timbers, common in the early 1800's to assist in construction. A lock on one of the doors was made in England and is dated in the 1830's. Interior walls are lathe and plaster with wainscoting . Cornices have dentil-like ornamentation in a sawtooth design.

When Samuel Burns, onetime mayor and alderman of St. Marys, purchased the house, he added rooms to the rear on both floors. In the 1880's, the kitchen was moved into the house, a parlor and porches were added on the rear and on the front across the full width of the house. The second floor was enlarged adding a bath and two small rooms on the back.

The dining room in the front section of the house built in the 1830's.

Heavy sharks-tooth cornice, chair rails, and a colonial mantle.

After the passing of Samuel Burns, his wife sold to Ria Rudulph in 1911, who built on the adjoining property and moved in there. She then rented the Bacon-Burns house. Tenants, in years to come, were the three Brandon sisters who later owned and operated the Riverview Hotel, and Burdette Loomis, a local entrepreneur who operated an early paper processing mill. In time, the house was converted into a boarding house and later an apartment house. In 1942, the house passed to Fernandina physician H. B. Dickens and later to Dr. G. W. Barker.

By the 1970's, the restoration craze brought W. L. Stucki to St. Marys. He bought the home from Dr. and Mrs. Barker and began a total restoration. The pine floor today is original throughout. The entrance door is at the center leading into an entry hall and center staircase to the second floor. To the left is the front sitting room adorned with fireplace and grand piano. The original ceiling cornice is highlighted with unusual sharks-tooth molding and the staircase is decorated with hand-tooled whale-tail brackets at the ends of each step level, both adding to a maritime theme.

OLD BARN HOUSE
OR THE OLD COACH HOUSE

The "barn" is somewhat exceptional considering its origin, being the gorgeous home that it is today. It was transformed to a home for the maiden Brandon sisters, Semora, Ethel, and Sally, in the early 1950's, then renovated to its present state by its current stewards in the 1970's.

The barn's construction is dated from the construction of home next door facing Osborne Street. The home and barn were owned by the Bachlotts. Their home was built in 1911. Mrs. Signora Bashlott was the married sister of the three maiden ladies. She and her husband provided the barn for its conversion to a retirement home for them.

The stately exterior holds little resemblance to this 'barn' of days of old.

Today's den was yesterday's stable and later an antique shop. Here were housed the horses, mules, and perhaps a chicken or two could be found balancing on a stall gate.

The rear staircase.

The living room was where the coach, buggies, and later autos were kept. There are two fireplaces, one on each floor, that are said to have been installed with the barn's 1950's conversion to a home.

FROHOCK HOUSE

The original columns and capitals were probably remnants of old structures being torn down on Cumberland Island.

In 1906, Lester Frohock constructed this spacious house by joining two houses from adjoining lots. Those two homes were of 19th century vintage, neoclassical design, one of which was purchased from the Rightmire heirs and stood three stories with a two-story porch. Wood pegs are still evident in both homes, indicating that their original construction dates could be dated to the mid or first half of the 1800's.

Lester Frohock included in his home, moldings, columns, and other timbers brought from buildings being demolished on Cumberland Island. He added a veranda around the east and south facades, supporting its roof with heavy ionic columns.

Frohock's occupation was as senior carpenter for the Carnegies on Cumberland Island. This afforded him access to an abundance of discarded yet still usable building materials. Much of that he recycled pursuing his second trade as an independent contractor in St. Marys.

The front sitting room embodies the period when families and friends gathered in front of the fireplace in conversation and companionship.

Decorative dental cornice and corner-blocked frieze molding surround the sitting room.

The morning sunroom was added by Lester Frohock for his wife who suffered from tuberculosis.

The entrance hall leads straight to the dining room and the front sitting room to the left. Traditional yellow pine is used throughout including the newel post, moldings, and floor.

Decor in the classic and Victorian tradition of today's interior.

The house remained in the Frohock family until 1953 when the house was purchased by Joseph Bauknecht who began various renovations which continued through the ownership of Lockhart family in the 1970's. The old plaster and lathe walls were removed and replaced, heart pine floors were refinished, breakfast and small utility rooms were added at the rear, and doors and moldings replaced as necessary. The four fireplaces were restored to working condition, and interior and exterior colors were researched to conform to the brilliance of the period.

The dining room is in the oldest section of the house, embellished with dental molded cornice and paneled wainscot.

Major Archibald Clark
*took his rank from his service in
the Georgia militia.*

JACKSON - CLARK HOUSE

In 1801, a local attorney and Revolutionary War soldier, Charles Jackson, purchased property on Osborne Street and began construction of a small home at what is today the south end of the house pictured above. Jackson unfortunately died that same October and the first floor of the house was only partially completed.

A young law school graduate, Archibald Clark, had arrived in the frontier town of St. Marys with his new wife, Rhoda Wadesworth Clark. He built a water-powered saw mill on Spanish Creek. Clark purchased the Jackson house, finished it, and, though detached, added the north end. Another detached building was added a few feet further north as the kitchen. It would later be joined with Clark's addition. It is still used for that purpose today.

In 1807, Thomas Jefferson appointed Clark Collector of the Port, an office he held under nine presidencies until his death. Although his chosen profession was attorney, he served as representative from Camden County and as a delegate to various state conventions. He was a member of the state militia and was

The Parlor is the only room in the house that still has the original plaster. The floors are what is called quarter sawn yellow pine, tongue-and-groove cut showing the finest of grain, six and eight inches in width. All of the wood in the house is believed milled at Clark's mill on Spanish Creek.

mayor of St. Marys for a number of years. His mill thrived and, over the years, Clark acquired great expanses of real estate.

In his law school days, Archibald had come to know Aaron Burr who went on to become vice-president under Thomas Jefferson. Burr was famous for his 1804 duel which killed Alexander Hamilton. Following the duel, Burr came south and visited with his young friend one night on his way to the Kingsley Plantation on Fort George Island.

During the War of 1812, invading British Admiral Sir George Cockburn confiscated the house for his local headquarters. The Admiral confined Clark to the brig on his flagship for failing to turn over a large amount of cash that the British knew he had. In later years, American General Winfield Scott was a visitor.

Major Archibald Clark died on December 26, 1848, and in the ensuing years, until this day, descendents of only two families have had ownership of the house.

This Federal style home, the oldest documented building in St. Marys, included a gabled, hip roof, pine-clapboard facade and a single-level front porch with a hipped roof. Originally there was a central hall plan within, which is now irregular due to additions in later years.

The dining parlor sits just behind the front sitting room and, as with flooring throughout the house, retains the original native heart pine.

When British Admiral Cockburn entered this room during their occupation of St. Marys during the War of 1812, he observed a rug in front of the fireplace that displayed the crown of England woven within it. The Admiral confirmed his observation of it to Mrs. Clark who responded, "Yes, and you will notice that we have it under foot."

The south wall of the sitting room displays a rosewood Steinway piano built in 1858 for Mr. Cohen, pioneer Jacksonville department store owner.

The guest room is where Aaron Burr slept for one night in late 1804.

Fireplaces that Clark crafted were state-of-the-art "Rumford" designed, extremely efficient in distributing a maximum of heat to the room. In recent restoration, mantles were removed and sent off to be stripped and refinished. Two-hundred years of heat on the brick had taken its toll requiring their replacement in all but one of the six fireplaces.

ORANGE HALL

Sitting gracefully on Osborne Street is found the architectural pearl of historic St. Marys, Georgia. The home takes its name Orange Hall from the "extensive hedges and the large sour orange grove at the rear of the house." This is a showcase of antebellum life in the Greek Revival style, with massive fluted columns below classic, yet simple, Doric capitals and triangular pediment. Its spacious rooms and wide hallways, and its garden's tree hedges all contribute to a simple frontier elegance. The architecture is, too, labeled a Doric prostyle temple. Its main floor is above the ground-level floor, the latter used primarily for food preparation, servant areas, and storage.

The property was originally granted to William Ashley, one of the founders of St. Marys. It later was owned by Phineas Miller, then Ethan Clarke by 1803. By 1826, Clarke sold this end of the block to John Wood and his son-in-law Horace Pratt, Pastor of the First Presbyterian Church of St. Marys. It is believed that construction began somewhere between 1826 and 1829, and perhaps lasted into the 1830's.

Conflicting stories tell of John Wood building the house for his daughter Jane Wood Pratt, while another tradition has Pratt building it for his second wife, Isabel Drysdale Pratt. Research by the Department of the Interior in the 1970's, speculated that construction on an earlier home may have taken place about 1830. It probably wasn't until between 1846 and 1853 that the larger and more expensive structure "was skillfully incorporated into the present structure..."

NORTH OR SIDE ELEVATION
Historic American Building Survey

152

In 1846, the property was sold to James Mongin Smith which, if true, would make Smith the owner when the present large structure was completed. In 1856, the home sold to Francis M. Adams, Mayor of St. Marys and the principal of a local academy.

With the American Civil War and the 1862 invasion of the area by Union troops, the house became headquarters of a squad of occupying troops and remained relatively unharmed. In 1866, it was sold to Elizabeth Ryals, the wife of a local attorney. She found a buyer by the end of the decade and it went to a New Yorker and became his winter home.

The grand old estate passed on through various stewards, each lending it their own degree of attention. The Beckers of New York bought in 1919 and upgraded the house to a state that made it the social center of St. Marys. The Fryhofers of Palm Beach bought it in 1925, but never lived in the house before selling in 1933. It was then converted to apartments to help house the many new residents arriving to work at the new Kraft paper plant. Orange Hall operated as an apartment until the about 1960 when its owner, St. Marys Kraft, deeded it to the City of St. Marys for use as a library and civic center. Today, the City of St. Marys perpetuates the grand old lady as a welcome center and living museum of the city's past.

Orange Hall has a basic four room, central hall plan with smaller rooms near the rear porch. Each of the eight major rooms is approximately 18 by 20 feet with 11-foot ceilings. There are two primary chimney flues, each being fed by six fireplaces, two on each floor, including the ground level.

At the left, and below, is the front parlor where music can be heard from organ or piano.

All doors and windows are pilaster framed with entablature above. Cornice moldings surround the ceilings and ten-inch baseboards are at floor level.

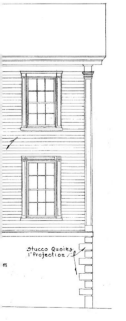

The charm of Southern tradition began at the grand entrance hall and its mahogany staircase that winds to second level in befitting grace. Treads, risers, and balustrade are crafted of the finest mahogany available.

A first floor sitting parlor, originally a bedroom.

The original dining room, now a sitting parlor.

At the top of the steps are found the children's rooms, spacious and open on one side of the fireplace allowing free access to an older sister's room. Molding and trim is much more basic in the children's area.

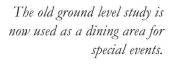

On the ground level is the kitchen, dining hall, servants' rooms, and storage areas. The hearth shown here is in the old servants' room, adjacent to the old kitchen and a similar large fireplace for food preparation. The hearth opening measures six feet in width and three feet, seven inches high.

The old ground level study is now used as a dining area for special events.

ROSE HOUSE

Concrete block 'stones' were and are an excellent insulation from excessive heat or cold, protection from severe weather, and are maintenance free.

The home was constructed in 1909 by D. P. Rose who was a well known merchant in St. Marys. Twenty years later, it sold to Dr. G. R. Thigpen, who owned it until 1956, when he sold to Rufus and Mildred Lovell. For many years it operated as an apartment house. It wasn't until 1994 that new owners restored it back to a single family dwelling.

The Rose House is esthetically unique in its use of formed concrete blocks as its primary building material in a community constructed of yellow pine. The contractor manufactured the blocks on site using molds, then cured and set the blocks. Three other structures in St. Marys were built using this same process including the knee wall around the community cemetery. Though unusual in St. Marys, the stones can be found in large numbers in cities such as Jacksonville. The roof is hipped with the front facade having a two-level porch, the second level having octagonal Doric capped columns on piers.

The house within follows the tradition of heart yellow pine floors, moldings, staircase baluster, hand rails, and newel posts.

The Rose house is indeed radiant from recent restoration.

The staircase from above and below showing the yellow pine floors and step pads and railings masterfully restored to their 1909 appearance.

STOTESBURY HOUSE

The Stotesbury House is one of the oldest of structures now standing in St. Marys. The first known sale of the property is documented to have been in 1791, and later, in 1818, it sold to John Stotesbury for $657 at a sheriff's sale with 'improvements,' implying that there was some sort of structure already on the property. The present structure, however, was built in 1821. In 1826, Archibald Clark acquired the property but it was later sold back to Stotesbury.

With the War Between the States, many of the homes were destroyed or heavily damaged. The latter may be the case with this house as, in February of 1869, the deed was transferred to Camden Sheffield for $175 with 'appurtenances.' Again in 1874, the deed was transferred to Charles Hardee for $500 with 'appurtenances.' In 1884, it sold to R.B. Sandiford, a local merchant and timberman, and remained in his name for many years.

Its architecture is vernacular folk Craftsman, one-and-a-half-story, side-gabled, side-hall plan house. Bay windows are on the west side facing Osborne Street, believed installed about a hundred years ago. There is a small stoop porch at the main entrance facing Bryant Street.

In 1992, the house was restored. Today, the lovely little cottage is maintained as a quaint gift shop.

Simple rosette blocks decorate the corners of each door and window casing.

Yellow pine floor boards vary in width from 3 inches to 8 inches, the wider being the older floors.

The old Stotesbury house is maintained today as the popular gift shop, 'The Blue Goose.' At the right is the kitchen, brought in from a separate outbuilding nearly a hundred years ago and retired from service when the 'Goose' was established in 1991. Narrow and winding steps lead to the one bedroom above.

RUDULPH HOUSE

This stately Neoclassical edifice was constructed in the 1850's for John Rudulph by his brother Frank Rudulph who operated the Rudulph Brothers General Store. The original structure was an I-shaped design, which was joined with a later addition making it a T-shaped floor plan. This provided each room with windows on three sides for excellent ventilation. On the front facade is a two-story porch with flat, Tuscan columns and turned balusters. The main entrance door and the porch door directly above both have transoms and sidelights. Two chimneys serve four fireplaces which heat the parlor, library, and bedrooms.

The old carriage house became a one-car garage on the south side of the house. In the rear was a hand-pump well and two-hole latrine that remained until utilities were brought inside. The basic house design today remains unchanged, a marvelous example of a comprehensive restoration work.

The house remained in the Rudulph family for nearly 90 years. Six generations lived here, the last being 'Uncle Joe' Rudulph who lived in the house for all of his 88 years, from 1878 to 1966.

Peering through the entrance hall to the parlor and eight-foot floor-to-near-ceiling-height windows. Transoms above the doors allow sunlight into the next room and assist with air flow.

The formal downstairs parlor is capped with the original medallion that once supported a beautiful chandelier.

A graceful walnut staircase ascends to the three bedrooms and veranda on the second floor while the entrance hall leads to the dining room and kitchen areas.

The *library* is basically unchanged from the early days of the Rudulph family .

The *formal dining room* radiates the moderate elegance of the antebellum South in tapestry, molding embellishments, and beautifully finished pine floors.

The Osborne Street facade with spacious porches and an excellent view of the harbor and a beautiful sunset.

SPENCER HOUSE INN

It was 1872, just a few years after the War Between the States, when William T. Spencer had this three-story hotel at Osborne and Bryant Streets constructed. Spencer, who was Collector of Customs, soon thereafter deeded the property to his brother, Stephen A. Spencer.

The building's architect and builder was Theodore P. Spencer, presumably a relative of William, who finished construction at a cost of $3600. It is a fine example of the Greek Revival style, with central gable, two-story porch with Doric columns on Osborne Street, and an internal central hall plan.

The Spencer was not the first hotel of St. Marys. Just east was the Ross Inn, overlooking Point Peter and Cumberland Sound. The Ross was believed to have been built in 1760, during the British Colonial days, and years before the town of St. Marys existed. The Ross Inn existed for some 200 years but was destroyed by hurricane Dora in 1964. The Spencer House, however, was the major hotel in the community in the late 19th century.

The Spencer House holds a prominent position in the history of community inns. The inn was purchased in 1889 by Daniel J. Long and his family, for many years providing visitors shelter in St. Marys when it was at one time the county seat of Camden County. The Spencer House was a favorite of Northerners who came for weeks at a time during the winter months.

The Longs operated a very lavish hotel, furnished with the finest of antiques, noted

Mike & Mary Neff collection.

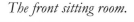
The front sitting room.

SPENCER HOUSE ST. MARYS.

From an ad that appeared in The Hotel Gazette of New York, circa 1877.

The Bryant Street Entrance.

The front sitting parlor connects to the central hallway and dining area.

Molding, trim, floors, and balusters are all painted yellow pine.

for the best of service. The hotel had a reputation and boasted the finest of everything. One visitor wrote that the immaculate hotel posted signs saying that they would not entertain guests who put their feet on porch columns or railings.

St. Marys Kraft purchased the building in 1941, using it for business purposes. About a year later, they sold it to the Westberry's who converted and operated it as a boarding house until 1982.

The building underwent extensive renovations in 1992 and 1993 under architect John Tuten, restoring it to its 19th-century charm, and today again operates as a favorite inn of the community.

Spacious hallways and staircase to the third floor.

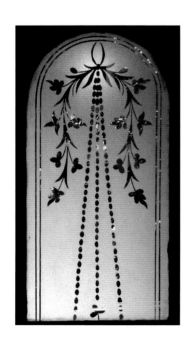

The Osborne Street entrance with frosted-glass door panel.

RIVERVIEW HOTEL

Small-town, old-South hotel tradition lingers on at the foot of Osborne Street. The Riverview Hotel was designed and constructed by J. H. Banks in 1916, for a corporation that included Mrs. Katherine J. Wadley as its principal. It was completed and opened in October of that same year. Hotel manager was George Johnson, brother of Kate Wadley.

The first floor rented to several shops. There was also a dining room, and living quarters for the innkeeper. For many years Bennett's Drug Store was on the corner where one could find all of the medicinal cures of the day or sit at the soda fountain and sip on a cherry soda. It is replaced today by the Cumberland Landing Cafe. Seagle's Saloon now operates where the hotel dining room was located. The second floor housed 20 guests rooms.

In the late 1920's, the hotel was purchased by Miss Sally Brandon, who, with her two sisters, Semora and Ethel, operated the hotel for many years, becoming a community gathering center widely known for its Southern style cooking and hospitality.

Through the years the hotel tenants have been a barber shop, antique shop, pool hall, and law offices. One claim to fame that came to the Riverview Hotel was the 1935 visit of cartoonist Roy Crane who stayed there and later depicted the hotel and town in his nationally syndicated comic strip, *Wash Tubbs*. Other visitors of note have been Georgia Governor Dorsey, author Marjorie Kinnan Rawlings, and Admiral Chester Nimitz.

The Riverview Hotel is a brick and block structure designed with two ground-level retail spaces, hotel lobby, offices, and on the second floor twenty rooms and eight bathrooms. Molding, paneled wainscot, and balusters are all heavily stained native yellow pine.

As with many of the old-time hotels of small-town America, the coming of the motel industry caused the Riverview to close, marking the end of a wonderful era. The Brandon sisters went into retirement, the dining room was closed, and the clientele and visitors dwindled to a trickle. The doors were closed in 1959 and remained so until 1975, when a great-nephew of the Brandon sisters restored the building. The classic old hotel reopened in 1976.

OUR LADY OF THE SEA CATHOLIC CHURCH

A bell tower was erected in the early years, but was removed in the 1950's for safety reasons.

Several French families arrived in St. Marys in the early 1800's and became the nucleus of the Catholic community. The James Vocelle and Louis DeFour families were among the first of the Catholic congregation.

The town of St. Marys deeded half of the southeast block of public square 89 to a Catholic congregation in 1826, but financially the small group was unable to build a sanctuary. A member of the Catholic group, Mrs. Maria Ponce DeFour, offered a room on the second floor of her husband's store as a house of worship. They met there for a number of years.

The Bank of St. Marys was chartered in 1818, but according to numerous local history sources, the building of its small structure was in 1838. In the 1840's, the little Bank of St. Marys failed, making the bank building available for new tenants. Mrs. Marie DeFour, who either acquired or already owned the building, verbally gave the Catholic congregation permission for its use. A steeple and bell were added in the ensuing years, as well as a picket fence that surrounds the grounds.

Damaged by Union troops during the Civil War, it was later repaired and remained in continuous use until the late 1950's when a new sanctuary was erected at Ready and Dillingham Streets. The little chapel today is used for special occasions with plans to reconstruct the bell tower.

The structure is a one-and-a-half-story temple-form brick building that is today the oldest masonry bank building in Georgia. It is unique in its simplicity, having no interior partitions or walls. Windows are sashed having stone lintels and sills.

CHRIST EPISCOPAL CHURCH

The earliest efforts to organize the first Episcopal church at St. Marys appear to have been in 1843. Local citizen Edwin Albertie conveyed a portion of block 42 in the Spring of 1844 to Wardens and Vestrymen of the Protestant Episcopal Church of the Messiah of St. Marys, the original name adopted by this small congregation. The original meeting place was on Conyers Street for about a year before the present site was purchased. The chapel built on the new property was constructed in 1845 and 1846 and is described as a wood structure with a steeple, interior blinds, and an organ. By 1850, there were 25 members attending the little church. The first pastor was Rev. Joseph A. Shanklin, and the first wardens were Miller Hallows and P. M. Nightingale.

When Union troops arrived in 1862, many buildings, including the small church on Wheeler Street, were fired on and destroyed. It was twenty years after the war before services were again held, then under the stewardship of Rev. Dodge of Christ Church at St. Simons Island. In the late 1880's, a second structure was raised. It was consecrated in January 1889. Local historians speculate that the present church structure was constructed in the early 1900's, though, due to the loss of church records, this can not be confirmed.

It wasn't until the 1930's that the name changed from Church of the Messiah to Christ Episcopal Church, believed a tribute to the rekindling of spirit and faith by Rev. Dodge and his St. Simons followers.

The present building is designed in the New England meeting house style with a gabled single-bay entrance porch with Tuscan columns, louvered belfry and short spire. Within, the ceiling is designed with exposed rafters, Tuscan pilasters, and a chancel, choir and vestry room added in 1914. One local historian rightfully suggests that the design of Christ Episcopal Church is "most suggestive of old St. Marys."

UNITED METHODIST CHURCH

In 1799, George Clark was sent "to preach and if possible form a circuit." That same year, John Garvin was appointed to settlements along the St. Marys and Satilla Rivers. Garvin, a young Englishman, reported fourteen members after a year's work here and along the St. Marys River. It would be, however, 1813 before the first Methodist church building was constructed at St. Marys.

The original Methodist church building was "a plain wooden building with slatted-back benches for pews," according to church historian Eloise Thompson Bailey. "The entrance was by two doors at the south end. The one at the right was for females and the other for males, as opposite sexes were not allowed to sit together." In 1856, a new church building was needed, according to church records, because the existing building had rotted beyond repair.

A new building of Greek Revival design was constructed by September 1858, when builders S. L. Burns and John Peal placed a lien on "the new Methodist Episcopal church and the premises on which it is erected for material and labor valued at $695." The very simple and small Basilicas-plan church was constructed of native yellow pine.

All public buildings were closed or destroyed during most of the Civil War but fortunately this structure was spared. According to local tradition, this site was used to butcher cattle.

Services at the Methodist Church resumed in 1866, and by the mid-1870's, membership had climbed to eighty-five. In 1892, the interior balcony of the 1858 building was removed and gas lights, a single-bay front porch, and a chimney were installed. The chancel was added to include two stained-glass windows.

Chancel windows added in the 1890's.

Windows are four feet wide by 12 feet high, each having 32 panes.

Nearly 200 years ago, eighty-three subscribers constructed a nondenominational chapel at a cost of $3442 on four acres of land donated by the town of St. Marys. The ladies of St. Marys donated $68 for venetian blinds, cushions, tapestry and various other trappings. The building was completed in 1808 and named simply St. Marys Church.

The original church entrance was on the east side (right side of the photo) which had a covered portico. There was an entrance on the north side (middle) for slaves or black parishioners..

By the mid-1820's, the Presbyterians adopted this original church site under the leadership of Horace S. Pratt, formally of New Brunswick, New Jersey.

Alterations and adaptations occurred over the years to conform to congregational needs and social demands. The main entrance on the building's east side facing Osborne Street had a double staircase climbing to a common landing at the entrance. This changed about 1898 when the original bell tower was moved from the building's north to the south side. The staircase and entrance that once led to the slave gallery was removed.

FIRST PRESBYTERIAN CHURCH

A devastating fire in 1956 brought statewide attention to the historic structure that prompted state consultants to report "the church is the finest example of early church architecture existing in Georgia." As a result of a state recommendation, a complete restoration of the edifice was accomplished to the specifications of the 1898 structure.

Today the First Presbyterian Church of St. Marys is the oldest structure in Georgia in continuous use as a church, and is the oldest Presbyterian Church in the state.

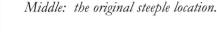

Middle: the original steeple location.

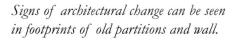

Signs of architectural change can be seen in footprints of old partitions and wall.

Chimneys Of
St. Marys

THE ROAD, FORT GEORGE ISLAND.

Scribner's Magazine 1877

FORT GEORGE Island

The steamer *Water Lily* makes daily trips from Fernandina to Fort George Island. Directly from New York, it takes four days of sea voyage bringing the traveler to the island by way of Charleston.... This paraphrased from the article "An Island of the Sea" published in 1877. It goes on, "Although man is here and there regaining the upper hand, Nature still claims the island chiefly for her own, and with that persistent grasp that never willingly relinquishes one inch where she has once borne sway, reasserts her claim wherever she can find the slightest hold. Over disused plantations she has called up a fresh young growth of trees and shrubs; over deserted and ruined buildings she has thrown a kindly veil of trailing honeysuckle and ivy; on felled and uprooted trees she has hung her soft gray moss, or has made the old prostrate trunk shoot up new branches in a young and vigorous life."

POINT ISABEL, FORT GEORGE ISLAND.

Scribner's Magazine 1877

Fort George Island, like Cumberland Island to the north, is a world unto itself. Facilities on the island are limited and access is by narrow, winding, and mostly unpaved roads. Peace, tranquility, and history are the island's primary assets. Fort George Island is secluded, hushed, undisturbed, serene, and full of peace. Its permanent residents are a scattering of private home owners, the U.S. National Park Service, the Florida Park Service, and dozens of wild peacocks and other species of small animals.

At one time, in the days of plantations and slavery, "cotton was king" on Fort George Island, wrote Harper's Weekly Magazine of 1878, but those days dwindled following the War Between the States. Bands of horses once roamed wild, as they do today on Cumberland Island, but all are gone now, removed in the late 1920's for their own safety. These wild horses were descended from the days of early Spanish occupation.

Following page: The Kingsley plantation house and Anna's kitchen cottage.

THE KINSLEY PLANTATION

THE KINGSLEY PLANTATION

Large bay windows had been installed, probably by the John Rollins family by the time this turn-of-the-20th-century photograph was taken.

The Kingsley house today is well preserved under the stewardship of the National Park Service.

Fort George Island today appears very much untouched by human indiscretions - lush in pine, oak, cedar, and tropical forest - hushed of the urban noise we have all unknowingly come to accept.

Archeological studies on Fort George Island have produced signs of human habitation that date back 3500 years. Most evidence of their presence appear as large refuge piles, or middens of discarded oyster shells scattered about the island. These are probably remains left by the Timucuan Indians, the island's native inhabitants.

In 1587, Spanish monks established Mission San Juan del Puerto near the center of the island. The mission was destroyed by South Carolina British invaders in 1702. In the 1730's, the British under General Oglethorpe, invaded the territory and, in June of 1736, built a fort on the island. Its location is believed to have been at what is referred to as Mt. Cornelia on the island's northeast side. The British successfully assumed control of Florida in 1763.

One of the first plantations on Fort George's Island was believed to be that of Richard Hazzard who was visited by botanist and writer William Bartram in 1765. Shortly thereafter, the lush island was granted to J. Tucker who raised rice and indigo on his plantation until about 1783, when Florida reverted back to Spanish control.

In 1792, Fort George Island was granted by Spain to one John McQueen who built a home and established a cotton plantation, known today as the Zephania Kingsley Plantation. The island house remains today as the oldest home in Duval County.

In 1804, McQueen sold Fort George Island and another plantation at Ortega to John Houstoun McIntosh for $28,000. John and Eliza McIntosh continued operation of the plantation, successfully producing crops of cotton and sugar cane. However, in 1814, the Spanish government expelled McIntosh back to Georgia for supporting efforts by Georgia-based interests to take control of the Florida territory in what was called the Patriot's Rebellion.

The Patriots had destroyed Zephaniah Kingsley's plantation called Laurel Grove at the mouth of Doctor's Inlet (now part of Orange Park, Florida). Kingsley was forced to move what he could to the protection of Fernandina in early 1814. Zephaniah Kingsley and his African wife, Anna, and their three children sailed from Fernandina

Florida State Archives

Plantation main-entrance door knob believed placed there after Zephania Kingsley's family arrived in 1814.

to Fort George Island in March of 1814. After renting the plantation from McIntosh for several years, Kingsley purchased the entire island for $7,000. Anna and Zephaniah raised their children at Fort George Island, and one child, John Maxwell Kingsley, was born there. They remained there until 1837, when American territorial racism forced their removal to Haiti.

The plantation remained in Kingsley's ownership until March 11, 1839, when he sold it to his nephew, Kingsley Beatty Gibbs. Initially Gibbs remained at his home at St. Augustine, using an overseer by the name of Charles McNeill to run his Fort George plantation. Gibbs was still active in politics and a variety of activities. In the early 1830's he had been appointed Clerk of the

The main plantation house was erected in 1798 on a coquina foundation above a basement. A central living room has two fireplaces and porches at the front and rear of the house. Rooms were built on the four corners with bedrooms on the second floor and an attic above.

A wing of the main house believed added during the Rollin's ownership.

Superior Court which continued to take much of his time. He later would write a journal of life on Fort George Island and of the day to day life there. His January 1840 entry tells of preparing the fields for cotton and, toward the end of the month planting sugar cane till the 31st instance. He made two or three visits to the island that month. On February 12th they began planting seed potatoes. On the 3rd of March they began planting corn, and on the 6th commenced planting cotton.

By late August the corn has been picked successfully and the slaves are out picking the cotton though caterpillars have done some damage. By October all hands were busy ginning the cotton, banking the cane, and digging potatoes. It was a good year at the plantation.

In 1843, Zephania Kingsley died and left one-twelfth of his estate to Gibbs. Shortly thereafter Gibbs purchased a parcel of land at the mouth of the St. Johns River called Hazard and built a lumber mill he called Mayport. That was the beginning of today's community of Mayport.

Gibbs sold his Fort George holdings on January 30, 1852 and moved back to his home in St. Augustine. The plantation and other nearby properties were sold to John Lewis for $12,500. The next year, it changed hands again, purchased by Charles R. Thomson who died a few years later. Charles Barnwell purchased the island and plantation in 1860 for $6280. It remained in his hands during the War Between the States.

The value of the property dropped to $5,500 by March of 1869, when John F. Rollins of New

Hamphshire bought the land to devote a large portion to agricultural production of orange and grapes, which was most successful in the 1880's and 1890's. To attract Northerners, Rollins built the Fort George Hotel in 1875, near what today is the site of the refurbished Timucuan Club. The yellow-fever epidemic of 1888, however, slowed further tourist growth on the island and most of northeast Florida. During the winter of 1894 and 1895, a number of hard freezes destroyed Rollins' Fort George Orange citrus trees and, most of all, the local citrus industry.

A highway was constructed to Jacksonville, in 1926, by millionaire August Heckscher from the south end of Fort

A second floor fireplace of the main house dating from the Kingsley era.

The fireplace where all of the meals were prepared for the owners and family. It was then delivered to the basement of the main house where it was warmed before being served on the first floor.

George Island, making it possible to drive to the island from the mainland for the first time. The Army Navy Country Club was established in the 1920's, later named the Fort George Club. They purchased and used the Kingsley Plantation house as their clubhouse. In 1955, the Kingsley Plantation house and the then abandoned clubhouse were sold to the State of Florida and became a state park. The National Park Service acquired the land and plantation house in 1991, and today it is maintained as a part of the Timucuan Ecological & Historical Preserve.

The barn constructed soon after Kingsley arrived.

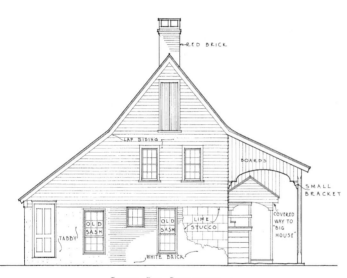

SOUTH END ELEVATION
Historic American Building Survey

The "Anna House" at the rear of the main house, was Anna' Kingsley's residence, and was where food preparations were made for the main house. The first-floor exterior walls were built of tabby brick and above, of wood framing. Here lived Anna and her children, George, Martha, and Mary, along with other of Zephaniah's "co-wives" and extended family members. On the south side of the first floor was the kitchen where slaves labored over large fireplaces before delivering meals to the main house.

A detailed view of a window sill and shutter on one building reconstructed by the National Park Service.

The Kingsley family had arrived from Fernandina on a flotilla of barges full of plantation supplies and slaves. The wood quarters that had housed some 200 slaves had been burned to the ground by rebels from the north, leaving only the main house to repair. During Zephania Kingsley's ownership, permanent slave homes were constructed that remain today, but in ruin.

Ruins at the south entrance road to Fort George Island speculated to have been constructed, but never completed, by Charles Thomson about 1855.

The interior of this particular tabby slave houses had two rooms. The picture at left is taken from one room, presumably a sleeping room, and looking into the living area that had a large fireplace for cooking and winter heat.

Scribner's Magazine 1877

Palms planted by Anna Kingsley and several of the slaves, assisted by the Kingsley children, created Palmetto Avenue.

Kingsley plantation buildings were raised using the abundant shells found in mounds left by the Timucuan Indians hundreds of years before. They were mixed with equal parts of lime, sand, and water and poured into wood frame molds. After hardening, they became the walls, remaining today in somewhat of a stable condition. Years after their abandonment, sections of the slave buildings were dismantled and used to construct other buildings.

Twenty-three tabby ruins encircle the entrance of the 200-year old plantation. They stand as a reminder of enslavement and forced labor in a turbulent period of American history.

Collection of Andy and Nancy Frashuer

Circa 1920's

JOHN STUART / VICTOR BLUE HOUSE

NELMAR CIRCA 1877

A kitchen wing was adapted to the west side of the house in the ongoing restoration of the house and grounds. Columns have been added that lend a Georgian Revival tone to the terrace.

A few hundred feet to the west of the house are the ruins of a two-story caretakers house, and just to the south is what remains of an indoor swimming pool.

Fort George Island, by 1869, had been purchased by John Rollins and Richard Ayer and within a few short years was subdivided by them for development. One of the first buyers, John Stuart, purchased property overlooking the east bank of the island and there built this broad shingle-style, two-story home. Stuart's daughter, Eleanor, married naval officer Victor Blue who graduated from the academy and distinguished himself in the Spanish-American War when he went ashore to reconnoiter before battle took place there. He later attained the rank of Admiral and, according to several sources, was the ranking officer at the surrender of the German navy at the conclusion of WWI. After 32 years in military service, Victor Blue and his wife returned to Fort George Island in 1919, where he became the major organizer of the Army Navy Country Club in 1923, later known as the Fort George Club. The club survived through the depression years, WWII, and a devastating fire, but due to a lack of patronage closed its doors in 1948.

The home's most obvious architectural signatures can be seen in its full veranda across the front and an abundance of large windows throughout the house. Its rooms are spacious and well lit from natural light. Fanciful and decorative moldings of the Victorian era during which it was built were not made a part of John Stuart's plans. The shingled exterior walls were popularized in coastal New England States on summer homes of the well-to-do who were looking for a rustic appearance.

The entrance hall spills into the front sitting room adding to the home's ability to entertain friends and guests on a grand scale. The east-facing side-lights and transom illuminate the entrance with the soft colors of morning light.

The second floor guest room affords a broad view of the landscape to the north and west. The multi-windowed, well-lit and ventilated design was very popular in close-to-the-seashore architecture.

The exceptionally large sitting parlor opens through double doors to the front veranda expanding the living area to the out-of-doors. Time takes its toll on the details of these treasures, as it has on the hearth tiles that await repairs, always ongoing in historic homes.

The thought of spider windows may seem somewhat eerie but add a bit of fascination to the long hallway that joins the four bedrooms of the second floor.

The staircase view captures the doors to the rear garden through a well-placed mirror.

- NELMAR -

The given name of the Stewart/Blue estate, taken from Admiral Blue's wife's nickname, 'Nel,' and 'Mar,' Spanish for ocean.

The barrel-arched doors to the family entertainment room.

BROWARD HOUSE

At the south end of Fort George Island, not far from the shores of the St. Johns River, is the Governor Napoleon Bonaparte Broward house. Though situated on Batten Island, it is at the entrance to Fort George Island and, because of its architecture and proximity to the water, it seems appropriate to tell its story. This Victorian vernacular is very typical of family homes in harbor-towns all up and down the southeast coast. What gives it that distinction is its widow's walk and cupola that crowns the hipped roof, allowing harbor pilots to see incoming ships miles out to sea.

Though this Victorian gem is located at Pilot Town, a community so named because of its early harbor pilot settlers, it was built in 1878 for a dentist, Dr. J. N. Gilbert. In 1897, it sold to the Honorable Napoleon Broward who was serving on the Jacksonville City Council, and was used as his summer home.

Broward, a controversial gentleman of his day, had been involved in gunrunning to Cuban patriots in their revolt against Spanish colonialism. This was a popular cause amongst many Floridians, one that was shared with Colonel Borden of Fernandina.

Broward served on the City Council from 1895 to 1897, was elected to the Florida House of Representatives in 1901, and was elected Governor of Florida in 1905. After one term, he was elected to the U.S. Senate but died before he was able to take office.

The exterior of the house has ornate sawed brackets beneath the eaves and between the columns on both veranda levels. The first floor porch was enclosed with screening years ago, but in a restoration begun in about 1997, the screens were removed and the second story gingerbread was replicated below.

The front sitting room. As with many homes of this age, the Broward house is in an advanced stage of restoration, the walls, floors, and fireplaces having received the best of attention.

The room layout is four rooms down and four rooms up. A kitchen was separate on the rear and at some point a porch was added. The ceilings are 11 feet in height and the front windows are sashed 7-feet by 2-feet, 9 inches with the original two over two glass panels.

Looking from the dock area, one can see the Broward house to the south, or looking north, Fort George Island.

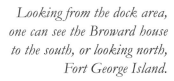

ST. GEORGE'S EPISCOPAL CHURCH

Nestled amongst towering palms on the island's east shore is the 19th-century Carpenter Gothic St. George's Episcopal Church. Typical of other small churches of the St. John River valley, the walls were of simple board and batten construction and a gabled entrance.

An Episcopal mission was established here in 1877 under the guidance of Bishop John Freeman Young, and, by 1881, funds were made available by a Mrs. Ellen Ward to construct the sanctuary. The building was completed and consecrated in 1884 by the Bishop of Florida, with beautiful stained-glass windows and the St. Agnes bell towering above.

St. George's Episcopal continued on for 113 years as a mission, until 1997 when the seventh Bishop of Florida recognized it as a full parish. A major restoration of the structure was accomplished in 1987.

The cupola or bell tower.

Nestled among towering palms and thickets of hardwood, St. George's Episcopal Church continues on with a small congregation of islanders as it has for more than 117 years. This is the second of only two churches known to have existed on the island, the first having been the Spanish Catholic mission of San Juan del Puerto, built some 300 years before the current edifice.

The sanctuary of St. George's Episcopal Church with open beam ceiling and simplistic St. Johns River architectural style.

Lancet shaped stained-glass windows of the alter wall.

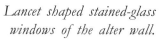

A gabled entrance with a simple pediment, a sharp roof line, and lancet windows all contribute to the little chapels 19th century Gothic architecture. The old shingled roofing has been replaced with stylish metal sheeting.

Low tide and the backwater along the west bank of Fort George Island reflects the late afternoon sun.

Sunset is coming on and the western sky illuminates the estuaries and the distant mainland.

MAJOR BIBLIOGRAPHICAL REFERENCES

Arnow, Isaac Flood. *Among Untrodden Ways: A Vignette of Delightful St. Marys, Georgia,* Madena Arnow Proctor, 1980.

Ballard, Mary R. *Robert Stafford of Cumberland Island: Growth of a Planter,* The University of Georgia Press, Athens and London, 1995.

Bailey, Eloise. *Orange Hall: St. Marys, Georgia,* The Orange Hall Committee, 1994.

Bailey, Eloise, and Marjorie Waters. *Historic St. Marys,* Gaule Tours, 1986.

Ballard, Julie. *Villa Las Palmas,* unpublished manuscript (date unknown).

Buchanan, J. T. *Our Lady Star of the Sea Chapel, 1840's, St. Mary's Georgia,* unpublished manuscript, 1996.

Camden County, Georgia, compiled and published by the Camden County Historical Commission, 1972.

"Catholic Church Has its Roots In 16th Century," *Camden County Tribune,* Kingsland, Georgia, June 19, 1986.

Corse, Carita Doggett. *The Key to the Golden Islands,* The University of North Carolina Press, 1931.

Cumberland Island National Seashore/Georgia, Historic Resource Study and Historic Structure Report: Historical Data Section, National Park Service, Denver Service Center, 1977.

Curtin, Cara. *Port of Fernandina: Link with the Past, Gateway to the Future,* unpublished manuscript (date unknown).

"Dynasty: A Florida Mansion Displays a Royal and Distinguished Past," *Country Inns Magazine,* May-June 1995, 40-47.

Fairbanks, George R. *History of Florida,* J. B. Lippincott & Company, Philadelphia, 1871.

Florida Masster Site File, Site Inventory, City of Fernandina Beach, Historic District, Nassau County, Florida, Sept. 30, 1985

"Forgotten History: John Rudolph House," *Camden County Tribune,* Kingsland, Georgia, date unknown.

"Forgotten History: Spencer House," *Camden County Tribune,* Kingsland, Georgia, September 4, 1975.

Fretwell, Jacqueline K. *Kingsley Beatty Gibbs and His Joujrnal of 1840 - 1843,* St. Augustine Historical Society, 1984.

"From Little Wild Horses to Fashionable Clubs," *The Jacksonville Historical Society Papers,* Volume V, 1969, 88-93.

Haase, Ronald. *Classic Cracker: Florida's Wood-frame Vernacular Architecture,* Pineapple Press, Inc., 1992.

Hardee, Suzanne. *Churches of The Golden Age of Amelia Island,* Amelia Island Museum of History, 1994.

_____. *The Golden Age of Amelia Island, A Glimpse, Second Edition,* Amelia Island Museum of History, 1995

"Hope Springs Eternal," *Water's Edge Magazine,* February-March 2000, 40-45.

Jaccard, Deon Lawrance. *The Historic Splendor of Amelia Island,* Lexington Ventures, Inc., 2000.

Johannes, Sr., Jan H. *Yesterdays Reflections II: Nassau Country, Florida*, Lexington Ventures, Inc., 2001.

Kummer, Julie Dressler. *Chadwick*, unpublished genealogy, 2001.

Litrico, Charles. *The Best of Amelia Now, Volume II,* Amelia Island, Florida, 2001.

Litrico, Helen Gordon, ed. *"The Palace Saloon, Where Shipcaptains Gathered In the Days of the Tall Ship,"* Land and Williams, Inc., 1981.

_____. Center Street Fernandina Historic District, Amelia Island Fernandina Restoration Foundation, Inc., 1976.

Mann, Jean Dixon, ed. *The Cemeteries of Amelia Island, Florida,* Amelia Island Genealogical Society, 1997.

McDill, Thomas C. *Willard's Mill and Other Stories,* Union County Writers Press, 2000.

Miller, Mary. *On Christmas Creek: Life on Cumberland Island*, The Darien News, Darien, Georgia, 1995.

Missionary Baptist Church of Fernandina Beach, Florida, Inc., 141st. Church Anniversary, unpublished church program, 2001.

Moore, Roger. *Amelia Island and Fernandina Beach.* Photographs Naturally, Inc., 2001.

"Pre-Civil War," Camden County Tribune, Kingsland, Georgia, July 5, 1979.

Proctor, Madena Arnow, ed. *Among Untrodden Ways*, self published, 1980.

Rockefeller, Nancy Carnegie. *The Carnegies and Cumberland Island,* 1993.

Schafer, Daniel L. *Anna Kingsley,* St. Augustine Historical Society, 1997.

Silva, James S. "Early Reminiscence of Camden County, Georgia, 1914-1915," *The Southeast Georgian*, date unknown..

Sickels-Taves, Lauren, Ph.D., and Michael S. Sheehan, Ph.D. *The Lost Art of Tabby: Preserving Oglethorpe's Architectural Legacy,* Architectural Conservation Press, 1999.

Smith, Ed *Them Good Old Days In Mayport and the Beaches*, self published, 1974.

Stowell, Daniel W, and Kathy Tilford. *Kingsley Plantation,* Eastern National, 1998.

"The Sea Islands*," Harpers New Monthly Magazine*, Harper & Brothers, 1878, 839-853.

Tobin, John, and Cory Tobin. *Historic St. Marys, Georgia,* River City Printing, 2000.

Torres, Louis. *Historic Resource Study - Cumberland Island National Seashore Georgia and Historic Structure Report - Historical Data Section of the Dungeness Area,* Denver Service Center Historic Preservation Division , National Park Service, United States Department of the Interior, 1977.

"Tour of Homes Saturday Highlights Town's History," *Camden County Tribune,* Kingsland, Georgia, April 22, 1982.

Wissinger, Joanna *Victorian Details*, E. P. Dutton, NY, 1990.

Wood, Wayne W. *Jacksonville Architectural Heritage: Landmarks For The Future, Revised Edition.* University of North Florida Press, Jacksonville, 1996.

Fort George Island's Kingsley Plantation and (right) the
Army/Navy Country Club, later the Fort George Club.